"Unlike many approaches that simply preach "spend less, save more", the Copperjar System™ will transform your relationship with money. It eases readers into rethinking their financial lives and empowers them to make the most of their personal finances with a practical, easy-to-understand approach. "

Don Roy, President,
University of Fredericton

"The analogy between the health management and wealth management professions is quite compelling, and this book does a nice job of flushing out what wealth can learn from health. As the saying goes: may you be blessed with good fortune and the health to enjoy it. The tools and techniques are similar."

Moshe A. Milevsky, Ph.D.
Professor, York University

"A practical, easy to learn and use process that will help you reach your personal financial goals despite the attraction of living and spending in the now."

Ken J. Killin, BBM CA, CEO of public & private technology companies

Also available in the Copperjar series of books:

The *Companion Workbook* for

The Copperjar System™
Your Blueprint for Financial Fitness

ISBN: 978-0-9866056-3-5

Available at:

www.copperjarsystem.com

or your favourite book retailer.

The Copperjar System™
Your Blueprint for Financial Fitness
(Canadian Edition)

Paul LaBarge

Alan MacDonald

Copperjar Group Corp.
Ottawa, Ontario

The Copperjar System™ is a registered trademark by Copperjar Group Corp.

Copperjar Group Corp.
138 Forestglade Crescent
Ottawa, Ontario, Canada
K1G 6A5
www.copperjarsystem.com

Ordering information
Quantity sales. Special discounts are available on quantity purchases by corporations, associations, and other groups. For details, please contact the publisher.

Individual sales. Publications by Copperjar Group Corp. are available through most bookstores and on-line book retailers.

Printed in the United States of America

Cover and interior design by VertexMedia.
Front cover image by VertexMedia. Copyright Copperjar Group Corp.
Back cover image by 123stocks, licenced by Shutterstock.com

This book is designed to provide information and guidance on the subject of personal finances. It is sold with the understanding that neither of the Authors nor the Publisher is engaged in rendering legal, accounting, or other professional services by publishing this book. The Authors and Publisher specifically disclaim any liability, loss, or risk which is incurred as a consequence, directly or indirectly, of the use and application of any of the contents of this work.

Library and Archives Canada Cataloguing in Publication

LaBarge, Paul, 1950-
    The Copperjar system : your blueprint for financial fitness / Paul LaBarge, Alan MacDonald. -- Canadian ed.

ISBN 978-0-9866056-2-8

    1. Finance, Personal. I. MacDonald, Alan, 1959- II. Title.

HG179.L3152 2010   332.024   C2010-903871-1

Table of Contents ———— -

INTRODUCTION

"You've just won $50 million dollars."

There are few of us who have not, at some point or another, dreamed of winning the lottery. Just imagine all that wealth. The ability to put an end, once and for all, to the constant quest to fill your bank account before the next series of bills goes through. Like the happy millionaires in the commercials we see on television, we could quit the rat race, present our loved ones with dream homes and luxury cars, and be free from the anxieties of managing our finances. Ongoing wealth and security would be ours forever.

This picture of financial Nirvana is created by lottery corporations in a bid to get you to buy another ticket to the next big draw. Somebody has to win, right? And even though you might have a better chance of being run over by a dump truck while swimming, you should go out and buy that ticket!

The actual experience of real-life lottery winners, however, stands in bleak contrast to the marketing pitch we're all so familiar with. Most lottery winners, for example, end up broke not long after the big win. Paul and Al have known four lottery winners over the course of their careers. Of the four winners, three are now totally broke.

You may think that getting rid of all that money so quickly would be just about impossible. Surely most winners are able to sock away enough at least to avoid going bust!

But lottery winners are not the only ones who burn through countless millions in short order. Consider all the professional athletes who show up in the paper a few years after their multi-million dollar contracts end, not because they're on the comeback trail, but because they've just filed for bankruptcy.

Then there are all those dot-com millionaires who burned through their brief bonanzas. Most of us have heard the warning "from shirtsleeves to shirtsleeves in three generations"—stories of family fortunes built in one generation, used in the next and lost in the third. It almost doesn't matter how much money you start with, if you don't have the financial discipline to manage your wealth, it will soon find another home.

As we battle our day-to-day anxieties about money, most of us give little thought to just how prosperous we are. All of us who live in the Western world at the start of the 21st century are the biggest lottery winners in history. The middle class of today is wealthy beyond the imaginations of 99 per cent of the people who have ever lived on this planet. Yet, in a recent poll, the number one concern of North American families is a lack of money.

This is because, despite our collective prosperity, we still share the same bad financial habits of the busted lottery winners and broke former professional athletes. On our own smaller scale, we spend more than we make, we acquire things that cost us money every month we own them, and we make financial decisions based on our emotions rather than using a disciplined approach that reflects our real goals and aspirations.

Sound familiar?

Think about it this way. Financial fitness has a lot in common with physical fitness. To achieve success in either takes a combination of good habits, discipline, the right information and a little skill.

This is a book about financial fitness. Its purpose is to give you the knowledge and tools to manage your money well, and achieve your personal financial goals.

As with physical fitness, the first major step on the road to financial fitness is to honestly assess where you're starting from. Are you financially out of shape right now? If so, what can you do about it? To fix a problem, you first have to face the facts and deal with them. Then comes the hard part: finding the willpower to change your current habits in order to reach your new-found goals.

YOUR BLUEPRINT FOR FINANCIAL FITNESS

There are some strong similarities between being physically unfit and being financially unfit. For one, neither state is immediately obvious at a glance.

For example, you don't have to be seriously overweight to be physically unfit. It is medically possible to be thin as a rail and still have arteries that are clogged with cholesterol. You can even have a physique that's the envy of the gym, and still not be able to engage in vigorous cardiovascular activity for more than a few minutes. The person who looks slightly overweight may actually be in better aerobic shape than his leaner companion, with healthier blood pressure, cleaner arteries and a less-stressed heart.

The same is true about a lack of financial fitness. You may have a fancy house, a stylish car, lots of snazzy electronic toys and an expensive lifestyle—but that doesn't necessarily mean you're really wealthy. You don't have to live in a trailer park to be financially unfit. The harsh truth is, that guy living in a trailer may in fact be *more* financially fit than you if he lives within his means, has a few dollars of savings and is debt-free.

If you can't climb a single flight of stairs or walk a few blocks without panting for breath, then it's fair to assume that your physical fitness may need some work. The same is true with your money. If you have to scramble to pay your bills every month; if you're living from paycheque to paycheque; if you're taking cash advances from your credit card and running outstanding balances; or if you have to keep dipping into your line of credit just to meet your current expenses—then odds are, financially, you're probably seriously out of shape.

Over the years that we've worked in the financial business—and between us, we have more than half a century of front-line experience with helping people manage their money—we've seen a lot of people go astray for want of a few simple tips and principles.

Alan has been a broker, banker and financial advisor for more than twenty years. Paul is a tax lawyer who has handled personal and corporate finance issues for more than thirty years. In all that time, we've had many a chance to observe human behaviour when it comes to money—to see the common mistakes so many people make, and to learn what can be done to correct them. Seeing the unnecessary carnage and misery that resulted from these mistakes led us to create a program that, if properly followed, will give you the ability and the tools to work your way reasonably painlessly up to a level of financial fitness that properly reflects your circumstances, needs, ambitions and means.

Like any other fitness plan, our system works by giving you the help and support you need to boost your own discipline. A good place to start is by being honest with yourself. If you're like most people, you probably aren't perfect. Believe it or not, neither are we. If you're in trouble with your finances, it's likely because you were a bit lazy or too casual about your affairs. You either knew the rules and didn't make the effort to follow them, or else you just turned a blind eye to the whole subject and hoped it would somehow work out for the best.

What you need now—what everybody needs when they first make a constructive effort to turn their lives around—is *help to deal with the problem*. Think of our program as the financial equivalent of Jenny Craig™, Weight Watchers™ or the YMCA. All those services are based on the simple reality that most people need the help of a coach to permanently change their existing habits.

We've named our program the Copperjar System™ after the jar that Al's grandmother used to put aside the family savings. In some ways, it resembles the workbooks we all used to have back in school. Think of these as *exercises* to get you back on the path to better financial health.

Some people may want to do these exercises and work their way out of their situations on their own, with no assistance. They just want a road map to point them in the right direction. Others may prefer to have ongoing help to check their financial "vital signs" as they go, sort of like a monitor for their progress. Either way, our step-by-step program is designed to be user-friendly—meaning you *don't* need a degree in economics or in-depth knowledge of the investment markets to understand the advice and benefit from it.

Most of us are familiar with the problems of losing weight, and with the best solutions to that problem. We have applied the same attitude to the challenges of trying to become financially fit. That's why, throughout this book, we keep comparing the process to a physical fitness program. (After all, that's a challenge that virtually all of us have had to address at some stage in our lives!)

So if you're serious about pursuing your goal, this book will help you get there. It's not fancy, it's not complicated, and it doesn't just hand out a bunch of glib tips of limited practical value. It doesn't provide a series of isolated exercises that only fix part of the problem. Nor does it start off holding your hand, only to abandon you when the going gets tough. Instead, this book offers a complete program to get you financially fit, which is based almost entirely on accumulated professional experience and a lot of plain old-fashioned common sense.

At each step of our program, we explain clearly why that stage is important, and we give you guidance to help you to navigate your way through it. The end of every chapter includes a summary of the key principles that have been covered, which are themselves gathered together at the end of the book into a handy "checklist for financial health." (But if you're tempted to just skip the next 140 pages and jump straight to the last chapter, be warned: that magic checklist won't make a whole lot of sense if you haven't read enough to understand its elements and how they all fit together.)

So be patient. It isn't a long book—we promise! As you read through each chapter, you'll find some tough questions for you to answer, and some tough issues for you to deal with. This book is meant to be read in stages and reread as necessary. Like life, financial fitness is a process. You can start, fail and start again, and still succeed in the long term.

To give you a rough sense of what you can expect, here's a brief summary of what follows:

- **Chapter One** helps you set your initial targets, goals and values, to establish the framework that will guide your decisions as you go forward. It asks you to honestly assess your current financial situation and attitudes, as well as how they affect your big picture. There's no single right or wrong answer to the question of how you spend or save your money. That depends on what's important to you. Your values aren't the same as someone else's, and their goals aren't necessarily your goals. The aim of this chapter is to help you focus on those elements, and identify what's vital to you and what isn't.

- **Chapter Two** asks you to undergo a "check-up," just as you would when starting a physical fitness program, to assess exactly how fit (or un-fit) you are right now. This baseline information will help you determine what your next goals should be, what kind of rigours you can withstand, and how much you should try to do in the early stages of your new fitness program. This chapter will give you a firm foundation on which to base your financial outlook.

- **Chapter Three** builds on that baseline and sets out the platform that will sustain your program going forward. The aim of this chapter is to get you to understand where your money is going, how you are spending it, and why you are spending it that way.

- **Chapter Four** allows you to set your own personal financial fitness goals for your life—long-term goals that include saving for your retirement, so you can sustain the lifestyle you want or imagine you'll want in the future. The object of this chapter is to help you take control of your financial future and get the advice you need to make the right decisions for you and your family.

- **Chapter Five** sets out the routine that will allow you to develop the level of financial fitness you need. This includes illustrating how you can start with a modest program, and build the confidence to succeed in your plan.

- **Chapter Six** addresses the issue of building equity. The aim of this chapter is to show that equity opportunities are everywhere, and don't necessarily have to involve putting all your hard-won assets at risk.

- **Chapter Seven** shows you how to trim the fat from your expenditures, and asks you to carefully examine your spending patterns and make any changes needed to ensure that your spending habits accurately reflect the new goals and values you've established for yourself. This chapter is about making spending a question of choice, not compulsion. By the time you've worked your way through it, you should be well on your way to being in control and conscious of how and why you spend.

- **Chapter Eight** is about understanding your limits and knowing what's achievable for you—and what isn't. Some financial programs promise the moon and instil false expectations, setting people up for failure. This chapter will tell you exactly how to deal with your individual circumstances in the context of your own unique reality.

- **Chapter Nine** brings together the big picture and provides direct advice and guidance with respect to the preservation of wealth and protection of your assets. It will help you learn how to protect and preserve the wealth you've worked so hard to build, both for your lifetime and for your children's.

- **Chapter 10** wraps up all the advice offered in the book, and summarizes (in that long-promised checklist!) the essential things you need to remember. This chapter says it all ... again. After all, it's your life. You own it, you can run it and enjoy it.

Let's be clear about one thing: this book is not about getting rich. There are plenty of other "experts" out there who are all too happy to tell you about their schemes for making a million bucks quickly and painlessly. You are quite free to listen to what they have to say. (Alan likes to quip that nobody ever "saves themselves rich." That's true, Paul says, but it's also true that nobody ever *stays* rich if they spend ill advisedly).

But in our 50-plus years of collective experience helping ordinary people manage their money matters, we've seen over and over again that there's simply no substitute for learning the basic lessons of finances. We believe that what's most important for you, and for every adult—old or young, male or female, rich or poor—is knowing how to create and sustain the resources you need to live well, live within your means and stay solvent throughout your life.

Although our topic is a serious one, there's no reason why it has to be boring. So we've tried to keep these chapters amusing as well as informative. That said, this certainly isn't the kind of book that's designed for light reading at bedtime or on the beach. It's also not one you can likely read right through at a single sitting. Make no mistake: there's a lot of hard work to be done here if you want to get the full value out of it.

But don't let that discourage you. Again, it's like an exercise program: what you get out of it depends on what you put into it. If you take a leisurely walk rather than going for an hour-long jog, you're still better off than somebody who stays at home on the couch. Similarly, if you can make your way through even the first chapter of this book, and it helps you refocus your financial priorities as a result of what you learn, then that's a major achievement!

With that one step, you'll be much further ahead in understanding your situation and making serious choices about how your financial life should be. The same goes for the rest of this book. Every chapter is designed to help you improve your financial knowledge and fitness.

Another aspect of the Copperjar System™ that we're particularly proud of is its interactivity. Information is available not just in this book but also through our website, **www.copperjarsystem.com**. We're trying to create a learning model that gives people a framework where they can learn how to handle and take ownership of their own financial affairs, in whatever way works best for them. It's about you taking control over an aspect of your life that you may feel is controlling you. Every success stays a victory for you, but each setback is just another lesson to be learned—and built upon.

If you read this book and want to let us know what you think about it, good or bad, feel free to contact us via our website and let us know your thoughts. If you disagree with anything we say, let us know. If you think it's great, we're pleased to have that feedback too. And if you have stories of your own to share with us and with other readers, we'd love to hear them.

We've worked hard on the Copperjar System™, and we believe in it. By the time you've finished reading this book, we hope you will as well.

One final note: we started to write this book just before the worldwide financial meltdown took place in 2008. At the same time that the markets were collapsing, Paul had to undergo heart bypass surgery. After his recovery, we considered whether we should proceed with the manuscript. After much deliberation, we decided that this book was even more relevant than ever. In fact, if anything, the meltdown in the markets demonstrated on an aggregate level what we had been talking about on an individual level for years.

The meltdown in the markets was a direct result of behaviours that collectively reflected exactly the types of issues that we have been addressing and will address throughout this book. The financial system was unfit. People had excess levels of debt, negative saving rates and wasteful consumer spending. The net result was that they were over-extended and unable to withstand substantial shocks and reverses in the market. Like some of the people whom we refer to in this book, they were making lots of money because they had to. They were over-leveraged, and they were making decisions based on the assumption that asset prices had no way to go but up.

Paul's bypass operation was as shocking to him as the collapse of the markets was to the rest of us. Before the surgery, he was generally physically fit, with good exercise and eating habits. But he suddenly found himself faced with the prospect of a quadruple bypass.

The reason in Paul's case was genetics. You might be tempted to translate that analogy to the argument that people are financially unfit as a result of their circumstances rather than their behaviour. While the circumstances in which we find ourselves are certainly important, we cannot overestimate the power of the choices we make and the actions we take to impact our lives for the worse or the better.

Paul's doctors, for example, made it clear that if he had not been physically fit, he likely wouldn't have survived to make it to the operating table. Paul's fitness also greatly shortened his recovery period, making it possible for him to get back on the road to recovery that much sooner.

We strongly believe that this is also the case when it comes to financial fitness. Being financially fit in bad times will enable you to withstand the shocks more successfully, and allow you to rehabilitate your financial future more effectively.

This book has definitely been an adventure for both of us, in terms of the experiences we brought to it, the process of putting it all together during the market meltdown, and Paul's cardiac surgery. The result has been both educational and entertaining. We hope you find that this book offers the same experience for you.

Alan MacDonald
Paul LaBarge

CHAPTER 1

Goals and Values

No one ever has a driving ambition to become overweight. Yet our society is still burdened with a growing obesity epidemic.

The most likely reason behind the mutual coexistence of these two, seemingly contradictory facts is that becoming unfit is a gradual process, which happens bit by bit over time while we're not paying attention to our health.

We can try to blame some of this on all the marketing that's pushed in our faces every day. Advertisers certainly love nothing more than to tell us what we should eat and drink, what kind of lifestyle we ought to have, which cars we should buy or what brand of beer we should drink—all the things that are important to a society characterized by conspicuous consumption.

If we're willing to be honest, however, we have to admit that the main culprit is really our own bad habits. Few people are willing to accept this responsibility. They blame their health (or lack thereof) on their busy lives, their stressful jobs, their genetic heritage and so on. But the bottom line is that, for most of us, our health is a direct result of what we choose to do or eat.

Money problems have a lot in common with the problem of becoming physically unfit. Most of the financial issues that people experience with debts or cash flow start gradually, as the result of falling into bad habits.

Little by little, unwise financial behaviours become entrenched in our lives. We succumb to marketing pitches, we give in to that relentless social pressure to consume, and we slowly slip into the habit of spending more than we can afford. In other words, we forget to keep our eyes on the prize: our long-term financial goals.

These temptations are a constant threat, which we will revisit frequently in this book. Because whatever excuses people may offer for why they have money worries, the truth is that nearly all of our financial problems begin when we start to get a little lazy about the basic principles.

The good news is, just as there are many things you can do to become physically fit, being financially unfit has a solution, too. Dieters often follow a structured program, not unlike the iconic 12-step program pioneered by Alcoholics Anonymous® and adopted by self-help groups ever since to empower their clients. What The Copperjar System™ offers is a "Nine-Step Program," which was created to help you achieve financial fitness and make your personal financial situation happy, healthy and robust.

Assessing Your Values

The first bedrock of a sound financial plan is learning how to identify and assess your core values as an individual.

People who are trying to improve their physical fitness often go on a diet, go to the gym, start losing weight and looking good—only to suddenly revert to their old habits, and put back on all the weight they've lost. They made progress, but they didn't change the underlying behaviour that caused the problem in the first place.

The same is true for financial fitness. True health requires not just a temporary diet and exercise program, but a lifelong change in behaviour. If you want the benefits to be a long-term, you need to change your habits for the long term, too.

To permanently change habits that are, for many of us, years or even decades in the making, you need a solid, practical understanding of your goals and values. Most of us rarely stop to think about our goals and values, let alone analyze and articulate them. Alan once spoke with a very dynamic couple who are involved in real estate. They are extremely successful, frequently ranking among the top realtors in the country. But when Alan asked them to describe their lives, they replied without a trace of irony: "We both work 12 hours a day, six days a week—but our top priority is always our children."

In today's hectic world, that kind of conflict between our goals and our values—in this case, financial success at the cost of family time—is all too common. The way we were brought up, the way we live, the pressures we put on ourselves and the artificial demands imposed on us by society—all of these affect how we view our lives. As a result, many of us have created unrealistic expectations of what's possible. Far too often, our behaviour is governed by trying to "keep up with the Joneses." We live out fantasies imposed on us by our neighbours, our colleagues, our friends or those omnipresent advertisers. In short, we create delusions about what we can or want to achieve. Then we spend all our time and energy pursuing those delusions instead of our own goals and values.

This was certainly the case with Alan's real estate couple. As much as they doubtless love their children, an impartial observer could be forgiven for thinking that their kids aren't anywhere near their number one priority when it comes to how the couple actually invests their time and attention.

This kind of discrepancy between our stated priorities and our real actions could even appear to be hypocritical. But it is our experience that most people, like this high-performing couple, are being completely genuine when they express their feelings. What we've found over many years is that such statements are truly **meant**, but poorly **executed**.

We have no doubt that the realtors really do consider their children to be their number-one priority. It's just that their lives do not respect their values. To put it another way: they know what's important to them, but they haven't quite figured out how to organize their lives around that knowledge.

Of course, few of us are lucky enough to have just one priority in our lives. Most of us have several or even too many, and we need to rank them by order of importance. When it comes to our careers, one fact that many people unfortunately overlook is that we're all usually happiest when we're doing what we love to do. That's the secret of successful people who enjoy their lives. The reality is, if you're doing what you love, just because you love it—then much of the time, strangely enough, your activities will be successful. You'll earn enough money from your labours to provide you with the lifestyle you enjoy.

Many people think of money as a goal in and of itself. In our experience, it's more like a yardstick that measures success. Money itself does not, as the saying goes, buy happiness (though it may make being miserable a lot easier to put up with). Sociological research has revealed that a depressing number of people (most of them men) work their whole lives at a job they hate, looking forward to the time they can finally retire and enjoy themselves. But a lifetime of bitter and grudging work may have so affected their health that, six months after that longed-for day finally arrives, they drop dead of a heart attack. What a miserable fate: to endure one's life rather than actually living it.

What causes this tragic degree of disconnect is a philosophy of "get rich at all costs." An astounding number of people have bought into this philosophy. As a result, they try to live out what's essentially a mirage. They create for themselves an expectation of how they ought to live, usually based on what they think others expect of them—whether it's their parents, their partner, or just the neighbour with the fancier car. The sad truth is that, emotionally as well as economically, many of us live in constant fear of having our secret inadequacies "found out" by others. So we end up spending all our time trying to hide behind the trappings of success. In the process, we put ourselves farther away from genuine financial sanity.

Identifying Your Priorities

Humans have a great capacity for self-delusion. Unfortunately, that delusion is what drives many of our worst decisions, financial and otherwise.

Many of us see a different image in the mirror than the one our friends and family see. One option is to try to conceal our flaws, so we can flatter ourselves that there's nothing wrong. The best solution, of course, is to make the effort to actually *become* the person we're pretending to be. In financial terms, this means developing a sense of economic worth that comes from the inside, not the outside. Becoming financially fit is something you do, not something that's done *for* or *to* you. Our goal is to help you focus on discovering the objectives that are most important to you as an individual, because they reflect your personal and unique values and goals.

In our long combined experience of working with individuals and businesses, we've found it's usually fairly easy for people to analyze their values. They just need to take the trouble to sit down and actually think about it. Our preferred definition for values is simply: "whatever you want the most." To put it in more concrete terms, think of the five things in life—they can be people, objects, relationships, principles or things, and need not necessarily have any cash value—that are most important to you. These are the things you'd instinctively grab if you had 30 seconds to flee a burning house.

Try it right now. Get a piece of paper, and write down the five things you consider most valuable. Your list might look something like this:

1)   Family first
2)   Family health (my own included)
3)   Financial independence
4)   Success at work
5)   Community service

These "most precious things" give you a reasonable steering principle for setting your goals. What's the difference between a goal and a value? Well, a **value** is what naturally powers a **goal**. For instance, if your value is "my children are what's most important to me," then your goal might be: "I want to arrange my life so that I can spend more time with the little tykes." A goal, in turn, should ideally transform into a concrete **action**. An action is something you actually DO to try to make your goal a reality. In the example above, it could mean cutting back on the number of hours you work, or scaling down to a smaller house.

How do we measure our values, goals and actions? Again, let's think of this in terms of getting physically fit. Most of us (those of us at a certain age and activity level, anyway) can relate to that kind of challenge. It's a struggle to get started, a struggle to find the time to keep at it, and a struggle to stay motivated. If you're serious about getting fit, the best way to deal with those struggles is to create and execute a firm plan. A plan can be as simple as buying a pair of good shoes and vowing to walk three times a week, or as complicated as hiring a personal trainer and a nutritionist.

For example, if your value is "fitness is important to me," your goal can be to reflect that value in your everyday life. Your plans might include "go to the gym every second day," "hire a personal trainer" or "make an appointment with my doctor for a complete physical."

Once you've decided on your goals and a plan to achieve them, write them down on a piece of paper and actually look them in the face. There's nothing more powerful than a clear set of values and goals, and there's something uniquely compelling about actually putting them in writing. If you can manage to complete only one exercise from this entire book, make this the one. Writing down your values makes them real. When you're clear about what's most important to you, you can set the goals you'll need to establish those values as the drivers in your life.

Let's take a look at a couple of examples drawn the list of values we drew up on the previous page.

Consider the value "**Family first.**" This value implies that whenever an important decision needs to be made, the first consideration should always be the welfare of your family. This may mean turning down a promotion that would keep you away from home too much, or rearranging your schedule to reflect your family as your first priority. A goal derived from this value might be "spend more time with my family." The specific action plan to gain momentum on this goal could be to "schedule a meeting with my boss to change my travel schedule."

So for this example, the **value** of "family first" translates into the **goal** to spend more time with your family, which leads to the **first action** of scheduling a meeting with the boss.

"**Family health**" was another value we listed. This value implies that you would like to be proactive about the whole family's health, your own included. This may mean increasing activity levels, changing your diet or reducing financial stress by moving to a more modest home. If the goal you establish turns out to be changing the family's diet, it might look like this: Family health **(value)** → change our diet **(goal)** = we will no longer buy soda or junk food **(first action)**.

A warning: setting goals may *sound* easy enough. But in fact, it's very common for people to get stuck at this point. In our crowded everyday lives, there are just so many competing desires, priorities and "necessities" that we want (or feel we ought) to do. You could even say that the process of setting goals is more about excluding those things that aren't truly important to you, rather than including the things that are. In a sense, it's a weeding out process, for separating the truly desirable from the merely tempting.

Setting Your Goals

Most people are driven by more than just financial considerations. For some it's fame. For others, fortune. Others still may crave nothing more than simple tranquillity and peace of mind. It is our individuality that makes this exercise so fundamental to understanding what motivates us. For most of us, our values accurately reflect who we are as a person and our real ambitions. But all too often, without realizing it, we let others set our goals for us. This can lead us to spend our lives pursuing things that we actually find relatively meaningless.

Some people, for example, sacrifice everything in the pursuit of wealth, ruining their health in the process—only to discover to their chagrin that all the money in the world can't make them healthy again. Other people cheerfully live on very little money because what's important to them is their art, their charity work, or just making it out to the beach every day in their quest to catch the perfect wave.

Granted, these are extreme examples. But think about yourself: where on that continuum would you feel most comfortable? Our society tells us that, by the time we reach our 20s, we're adults, our characters set and our education over. But the psychological reality is that we continue to grow and change throughout our lives. We're influenced by all the things we learn or are taught through the decades. By the time we hit our 40s, we often look back on our life experience and begin to question the assumptions that have guided our behaviour for so long.

Try this exercise: without thinking about how realistic or attainable they are, take a piece of paper and make a list of 30 things you want to *have* or *do*. They can be material things (that plasma TV you've been hankering for), immaterial (a healthier relationship with your spouse or sibling), romantic (a second honeymoon in Venice), recreational (a better golf swing) or idealistic (a better world for your children to live in). The important thing is to write them all down in whatever order they occur to you, and try to be as specific as you can.

(We'll take a pause while you write that list. No cheating, and no promising to "go back and do it later!" Remember, to get the most out of this section, you have to focus on it.)

Your list of 30 things may look something like this:

1)   Learn to fly.

2)   Take the family to the beach.

3)   Run a marathon.

4)   Lose 30 pounds.

5)   Take my spouse to Venice.

6)   Get a new car.

7)   Get promoted at work.

8)   Grow my savings to $500,000.

9)   Take six weeks of holidays.

10)   Go back to school and finish my degree.

11)   Walk my kid to school every morning.

12)   Give away $10,000 to my favourite charity.

13)   Buy a whole new wardrobe.

14)   Coach my daughter's soccer team.

15)   Learn yoga.

… and so on, until you get to a list of 30 wishes and wants.

Now that you have your list, the next step is to turn them into workable goals. If you really look them over, you may realize that some of the things on your list are really different aspects of the same goal. For example, if you've written "lose 10 pounds," "reduce stress" and "improve my tennis serve," you can probably group all of these goals under the general heading of "increase my fitness."

In fact, if you're like most people, your goals—no matter how disparate they may seem at first glance—likely fall into a small number of broad categories, such as home improvement, personal relationships, leisure activities, professional development, community involvement and so on. Many people find that their 30 items fit comfortably into five or six such groups, and these groups probably represent the top priorities in your life right now.

One of the most useful things about turning your wants and wishes into goals, is that goals can be measured. This takes them from the vague limbo of "I really ought to get fitter" to the firm foundation of "by next summer, I want to be able to run five kilometres without passing out." Goals spark action, and action is quantifiable. In addition, actions usually tend to lead to more action. We just need to take that first step, and more often than not, the other steps will quickly fall into line.

A respected mentor whom Alan has known for many years likes to call this initial spark the "first potato chip," because you can't stop at just one. When it comes to exercise, for instance, your first potato chip could be something as simple as putting on your gym shorts three times a week. Usually, the mere act of wearing the shorts will put you in the right frame of mind to exercise (your second potato chip), and you'll end up doing at least a few pushups or a walk around the block (the whole bag!). Once you've progressed a little, you may decide to hire a trainer. If you've scheduled and paid for a session, you will be much more motivated to show up and go through the motions of exercising. And when it comes to exercising, motion is what counts!

Let's try a little exercise of our own. In the following table are examples of five hypothetical goals. Look them over, and then use the same format to make a table for your own list of goals. This table will lay the foundation for your personal action plan.

Goal	3-Year Result	1-Year Result	"First Potato Chip"	How/ Where To Measure
Improve personal fitness	I will have 15% body fat and run three 10k races per year.	I will have 20% body fat and exercise three times per week.	Hire a personal trainer.	My workout schedule will be posted on the fridge.
Increase time spent with family	My husband and I spend four nights per week at home and organize an annual family vacation.	I have scheduled my four weeks of vacation for the coming year.	Schedule a meeting with my boss to discuss my travel schedule.	In my work organizer.
Aim for financial independence	I earn more than I spend.	I know what I spent last year.	Do a cash flow analysis.	On my Copperjar System™ cash flow worksheets.
Engage in community service	I spend five hours per month on community service and give $4,000 to charity.	I have joined the volunteer committee at my church.	Call my pastor.	In my work organizer.
Undertake professional development	I will have my industry certification.	I have completed my first course.	Register for the online course.	In my work organizer.

Coordinating With Family

When it comes to analyzing our values, setting goals and putting changes into action, it's important to remember that few of us have the luxury of acting with complete independence. We have to consider other people's wishes and needs—most importantly, those of our family.

As we write this, there is a television ad running in frequent rotation that shows a middle-aged couple consulting with a financial advisor about their retirement. The husband is enthusiastically talking about his vision of relaxation: reading the paper, basking in the sunshine, stopping to smell the roses and just generally enjoying the peace and quiet of retirement. Meanwhile, his wife is sitting behind him holding up a series of cue cards for the advisor illustrating what *she* wants from retirement: travel, shopping, wining and dining, a whirlwind of energy and spending money.

It's an amusing ad, but it pinpoints a familiar reality of family life: people may automatically assume they're on the same page, when in fact, their visions for the future can be miles apart. This doesn't necessarily mean there's a lack of communication between married couples. It simply addresses some fundamental issues about relationships—namely, that two people can have very different goals, yet those differences can go unspoken and unheard for many decades of financial togetherness. The divergence has to be addressed, since it has an impact on both how they live and how they arrange their finances.

While we encourage you to analyze your personal values and goals, it is equally important to understand that, when we belong to a family, we're team players. You need to know what the team needs from you, what you need from them, and how to reconcile your own goals with the team's objectives. If you don't tackle this issue you could end up, like the couple in the ad, pulling in two different directions.

Paul was once negotiating with a fellow in Atlanta who had a very colourful way with language. When Paul suggested something to him, he responded: "That dog won't hunt." After Paul stopped laughing, he thought about how accurate an assessment that was of certain situations. Figuratively speaking, how often in our lives do we set out on a "hunting trip" with a "dog" that just isn't up to the task? When it comes to family finances, divergence between partners is a classic "dog that won't hunt."

We recommend that you and your partner do these exercises, if not together, then at least in consultation with each other. If you've already listed your own values and goals, for example, the next step is to talk them through with your partner to see how your visions compare. In most cases, we've found that couples who take the time to discuss this subject discover that their goals are virtually identical (at least in the broad outline, if not always in the fine details). If that's your case, then you're ready to finish this chapter and move on to the next. Those couples who have significant differences, frequently have much larger issues than their finances.

If your goals don't converge, or if you have quite different values, this might be a good time to discuss how you can bring your goals into alignment, or how you can manage to meet both sets of goals. Don't be afraid to get professional counselling. After all, you'll find it a lot easier to achieve your objectives if you're working together rather than against each other. And once you're armed with a clear vision of your values and goals, you've already come a long way financially— much farther than most people ever will. You should congratulate yourself on that accomplishment before moving on to the rest of the book.

To begin a values and goals conversation with your partner, try asking yourselves the following questions:

How do you see yourself 10 years from now?

a) Where are you living?
b) What are you doing?
c) How much do you earn?
d) What roles do you occupy in your family's lives?
e) How do you want to be financially? (Examples: mortgage paid down or off, debt-free or with less debt, $500,000 in investments, etc.)
f) What community service do you want to achieve?
g) What are your spiritual goals?
h) Is there anything else that comes to mind?

This is an exercise to get you thinking forward, so it doesn't have to be precise. Just be sure to talk it over with your partner, and as always— make sure to write down your thoughts.

Summary of Chapter One

- Financial fitness is like physical fitness: it's something that **you** do, not something that's done *to* or *for* you.
- The best definition of "values" is "the things that are of greatest importance to you."
- **Goals** are useful to plan **actions**. Often our lives are motivated by what we think other people expect of us, such as friends, family members or advertisers who only want us to buy stuff. Having clear goals helps you put your own values first.
- Write down your values and goals using the exercises provided here. Then find that "first potato chip" that gets you moving.
- If you're a member of a couple or family, your values and goals should converge with those of your spouse or partner. Share your thoughts and feelings, and respect each other's differences of opinion.

To get the most out of this chapter, complete your own list of five key goals. One way to ensure your five-goal list reflects what is most important to you is to start off with writing out 30 things you would like to do or have. Write the 30 wants and desires without thinking too much about whether they are practical or when you might do them. Just write out whatever comes to mind. For example:

1) Learn to fly.
2) Lose some weight.
3) Go on a family vacation.
4) Finish my degree.
5) Run a 10k race.
6) Go out once a week with my husband.
7) Spend one night a week with each of the kids.
8) Get a promotion at work.

9)   Learn to play the piano.

10)   Buy an investment property.

11)   Pay off my credit cards.

12)   Save money every month.

13)   Get off my blood pressure medication.

14)   Volunteer at the hospice.

15)   And so on....

Once you have your 30 items, you will likely find that some of these things are actually parts of a larger goal. See if you can reduce your list to five key priorities or measures. You can do this on a piece of paper or you can use the template you'll find at **www.copperjarsystem.com.** Your list of five key goals might look something like this:

Goal	3-Year Result	1-Year Result	"First Potato Chip"	How/Where To Measure
Improve personal fitness	I will have 15% body fat and run three 10k races per year.	I will have 20% body fat and exercise three times per week.	Hire a personal trainer.	My workout schedule will be posted on the fridge.
Increase time spent with family	My husband and I spend four nights per week at home and organize an annual family vacation.	I have scheduled my four weeks of vacation for the coming year.	Schedule a meeting with my boss to discuss my travel schedule.	In my work organizer.
Aim for financial independence	I earn more than I spend.	I know what I spent last year.	Do a cash flow analysis.	On my Copperjar System™ cash flow worksheets.

Goal	3-Year Result	1-Year Result	"First Potato Chip"	How/Where To Measure
Engage in community service	I spend five hours per month on community service and give $4,000 to charity.	I have joined the volunteer committee at my church.	Call my pastor.	In my work organizer.
Undertake professional development	I will have my industry certification.	I have completed my first course.	Register for the online course.	In my work organizer.

CHAPTER 2

Your "Financial Fitness" Check-Up

Imagine you're a fairly sedentary person who has decided to finally get into shape. If you go to the gym, you'll see warning stickers on all the weight machines saying things like "See your doctor before starting an exercise program" or "Stop exercising immediately if you feel faint or dizzy." Those notices are there for two reasons: first, the makers of the equipment really prefer that you *don't* have a heart attack and die on one of their machines; second, if you choose to ignore the warning and overstress yourself anyway, they don't want to be sued by your grieving family.

When it comes to recreation-related injuries, the people who most often get themselves into trouble are the weekend warriors—men and women (though mostly men!) who are so passionate about their sport that it leads them to pry their middle-aged, less-than-fit carcasses off the couch every few weeks to strap on their gear and head out for a "friendly" game. Unfortunately, these friendly games can be the worst sort of activity for those who are not physically fit. The pace is frenetic, and it is athletically demanding, but only in brief spurts—precisely the kind of activity that poses the greatest risk for anyone whose lifestyle or family history make them prone to cardiac events.

As a result, when weekend warriors behave like they're trying out for the pros, they experience a disproportionate number of heart attacks. This sad phenomenon has become so common that many sporting facilities around the country have had to install cardiac defibrillators as a regular piece of equipment. Like the signs on gym machines, the presence of a cardiac defibrillator is a warning: know what a reasonable starting point is for you, and know your limits, or be prepared to pay the price. If you ignore these warnings, you're being at best haphazard about your fitness goals and, at worst, downright reckless.

If you want to improve your fitness—physical or financial—the best way to begin is to seek out sound advice from a skilled professional. When you start an exercise program, your first step should be to consult your doctor, who'll assess your current state of fitness and tell you what's a reasonable activity level for you to start with. You won't stay at that level forever, but you should certainly use it as a safe base from which to work your way up.

It's the same with financial planning. Many (if not most) "do it yourself" approaches don't work very well, for one very simple reason: they focus so much on distant goals that they forget about their starting point today. Yes, where you want to get to is certainly important; but equally vital is where you are right now. Just like building a house, the foundation has to come first. Despite this, conventional financial plans often spend very little time working out what kind of a base you have to build on.

Most DIY financial plans, for instance, tend to start at the end and work backwards. For instance, an advisor might calculate your supposed retirement or estate needs, based on a certain set of assumptions, and then tell you exactly how much you need to save to enjoy a particular lifestyle for the rest of your days. You take one look at the huge number their software program has calculated, nod in agreement—and then as soon as you get home, you toss the plan in the trash. It looks totally hopeless and completely unrealistic, so why even bother trying?

The difference between this type of planning and a real financial fitness plan is the same as the difference between the latest fad diet and a true, lifelong change in eating and exercise habits. One will probably last about three weeks before you end up falling off the wagon. The other is a proven approach that is based on sound nutritional information, and which really *does* empower motivated people to shed their excess pounds.

"A Minute on the Lips, a Year on the Hips"

That's how diet gurus warn you about yielding to the delicious temptation of that Double Fudge Chocolate Brownie. Is the brief pleasure of a sinful dessert really worth the sacrifice of your long-term goals?

It's the same with financial goals. In North America, sadly, the marketing industry is largely designed to siphon off your wealth as quickly as possible. Taken to the extreme, it may even deprive you of your future ability to create wealth. This is done with just one purpose in mind: to provide YOU with instant gratification and provide THEM with your hard-earned cash.

Let's face it: we're all more influenced by advertising than we'd like to believe. And advertising (unless it's for pharmaceuticals, with their rapid-fire listing of possible unpleasant side effects) is all about the positives, not the harsh realities. We don't know about you, but we've never seen an ad for a credit card company that showed their collection agency sending threatening letters, banging on your door or threatening to evict you from your home.

In our modern consumer society, the plain fact is that buying is an emotional activity. It feeds our needs, comforts our insecurities and gives us immediate gratification. Merchants and marketers know this better than anyone, and they deliberately design their ads to appeal to those emotional needs.

By contrast, actually paying for our indulgences is much less emotional. It's a rational and conscious thought process. As such, it tends to kick in only a long time after we have acted on our feelings.

Balance Sheets and Cash Flow

The best tool in your arsenal to defend against these temptations is information. To avoid the financial equivalent of a heart attack, when you start a financial fitness plan, you need to become informed about your current finances—and you need to go slowly.

The ground rules are simple:

- Realistically assess where you are today and what your "starting level" is;
- Analyze what you spend your money on right now;
- Put together a detailed balance sheet of what you own and what you owe;
- Spend some time imagining the lifestyle that you'll want to lead in the future;
- Get skilled professional advice, the financial equivalent of a visit to your doctor; and
- Based on all of the above, create a realistic set of goals that you can work towards—goals that will actually motivate you, rather than program you for failure or cause you to quit before you really begin.

Accountants do these sorts of plans for businesses all the time. In fact, one of their main functions is creating cash flow statements and balance sheets. A skilled accountant or financial analyst can take one look at a company's cash flow statement and balance sheet, and know everything there is to know about the organization's financial health.

The same is true for individuals. Your cash flow and balance sheet can tell you and your advisor everything you need to know about your current financial health.

Tracking the Elusive Cash Flow

When it comes to cash flow, only two numbers matter. The first is how much money you bring home. The second is how much you spend.

All of your future financial joy or despair, success or failure, depends on which number is bigger. If the answer is the first, you're in good shape. But if it's the second, you might want to check around for the nearest cardiac defibrillator, because your game plan is taking you in the direction of a financial heart attack.

To avoid picking on our clients—and to show you that even financial advisors are human when it comes to money—let's use ourselves as an example. Alan used to think he had a pretty good handle on his monthly spending. He made lots of money as an investment advisor, and he, his wife and their two kids lived quite comfortably in a nice area. Their bills always got paid on time, and things seemed to be taking care of themselves.

But some things still had him puzzled. In spite of steady increases in his earnings, for instance, there never seemed to be much extra cash kicking around. Investments were always stuck in the category of "we'll get around to it some day." Their house was going up in value, true; but so was their line of credit. Perhaps most tellingly, they'd stopped paying off their charge cards in full at the end of each month. In other words, things were going a bit off-kilter.

So Alan bit the bullet and decided that if he was going to advise others on their finances, he had better get his own financial house in order first. Getting down to the task was heavy going—in large part because, at that time, nobody had yet written a book like this to simplify the topic. Conventional books on financial planning always seemed about as useful as Olympic training tips to a confirmed couch potato. So Alan decided to start by checking his cash flow. He pulled out all his bank and credit card statements, set up a spreadsheet and began adding up how much he spent every month, where, and on what.

CHAPTER 2: YOUR "FINANCIAL FITNESS" CHECK-UP

The results were shocking. Alan found that, every single month, he was spending close to $3,000 more than he earned. How was it possible for *anyone* to be that far out of whack, and not be aware of it—least of all someone who calls himself a financial professional?

The answer is a simple one, for pros and amateurs alike. Overspending is a lot like gaining weight. You don't go to sleep one night lean and fit, and wake up the next day 50 pounds heavier. We get heavier an ounce or so at a time, in small increments that seem unimportant at the time: a celebratory dinner here, an extra helping of pasta there, a once-a-week breakfast Danish that becomes a daily habit, or a gradual dropping of the daily brisk walk in favour of watching an extra hour of TV. It happens so gradually that we don't even notice it until our pants suddenly don't fit anymore, and even then, we often decide that it must be the dryer that's shrinking them.

Financially, we do exactly the same thing: eating out, ordering in, new cell phone plans, the dog's surgery, the kids' braces, the timeshare condo in Aspen that seemed like such a steal, the new work wardrobe, little Johnny's new sports equipment... little by little, without realizing that our spending is overtaking our earning, we wind up in debt. To make matters worse, our credit-happy society offers us all kinds of holes in the sand where we can happily bury our heads and kid ourselves about how things really stand.

Loans are one of the biggest thieves of our resources. Our houses can usually be counted on to appreciate in value, so it's always easy to dip into that line of credit—not too much, just $20,000 here for a new pool or $30,000 there to consolidate the credit cards. We're still earning a good salary, so this isn't really a big problem, right?

Wrong. If that's the situation you're in—as Alan was back then, and as so many people are every day—then you're standing on a financial slippery slope that ends right at an economic cliff. The time to check whether or not you're being financially responsible is right now, this minute. Only when you have an accurate understanding of your cash flow today can you start to plan rationally for tomorrow.

But what about Paul? Were his finances in better shape? In contrast to Alan, Paul and his wife were more cautious personal spenders. They reviewed their finances regularly, established a budget and decided how much they could spend per month on each aspect of the household. They physically placed those predetermined amounts of cash into envelopes labelled things like "Bills," "Groceries," "Gas" and "Entertainment."

As a system, this is foolproof: when an envelope was empty, Paul just stopped spending until it was time to fill it up again. Now he uses dedicated bank accounts to do the same thing. The beauty of this approach is that there's no way for even the most in-denial spender to keep fooling himself with multiple lines of credit, or balances transferred from one place to another. In other words, it enforces virtue—as long as it's used regularly. Paul abandoned the system for a brief time after his banker suggested consolidating all his accounts. To his chagrin, he soon found himself sliding down the same slippery slope as Alan, indulging in untracked overspending.

We needn't all resort to Paul's envelope system, but there are other approaches available for keeping track of earning versus spending. Many people swear by commercial software like Quicken® or Microsoft® Money (which have the added benefit of making tax-time a little easier). It doesn't really matter which method you use. What's vital is that you know whether you are spending more than you make, and how you are spending it. This knowledge is the indispensable foundation of your personal economic well-being, and the basis for all rational future planning.

Which Number is Bigger?

So how can you reliably figure out exactly how much you are spending, where your money is going and whether or not you're headed in the right direction? As we discussed earlier, there are basically two essential tools for this job: a cash flow spreadsheet and a balance sheet.

It doesn't really matter what format your cash flow statement takes, but if you don't already have a spreadsheet handy, you'll find a straightforward, easy-to-use one on our website at **www.copperjarsystem.com**. Some cash flow models are way too complicated, so we prefer a simpler, no-frills tool that doesn't take a certified accountant to use. Just enter the information from your bank and credit card statements into the blanks each month, and let the spreadsheet do the rest. It's a painless way to answer your most important ongoing financial question: "How am I doing?"

A basic personal cash flow statement will look like something like this:

Cash flow for the month of June:

Cash in:

Net income first income earner:	$4,200
Net income second income earner:	$3,200
Refunds from health plans/stores:	$350
Total cash in:	**$7,750**

Cash out:

Savings:	$1,200
Charitable contributions:	$200
Insurance:	$425
Utilities:	$600
Phones, cable, Internet:	$225
Mortgage:	$655
Taxes:	$450
Car expenses:	$800
Groceries:	$550
Restaurants/entertainment:	$540
Household expenses:	$345
Clothing:	$235
Travel:	$450
Childcare:	$500
Healthcare:	$450
Total cash out:	**$7,625**

Cash Flow = Total cash in – Total cash out = +$125.

A balance sheet is a bit different. It divides all your finances into two categories: **assets** and **liabilities.** Assets are the things you **own** that are worth money. Liabilities are your debts, or what you **owe** to others.

Lining these two columns up next to each other can be a sobering experience. Numbers don't lie, and they make it impossible to avoid acknowledging that you're not only unwittingly spending more than you make, but you may also *owe* more than you *own*. Though a simple piece of paper can be the basis for a perfectly effective balance sheet, we're partial to the handy Copperjar System™ version available on our website. You can either print out a hard copy, or let the online version add up the numbers for you at the click of a mouse.

However you go about it, it's important to establish this vital benchmark before you go any further. A balance sheet doesn't have to be accurate to the penny, or even to the nearest hundred dollars. Feel free to approximate the value of your house and personal effects. Just remember to use their current or resale value, not what you originally paid for them. By now, that $10,000 oak bedroom set would net you maybe $1,500 tops if you sold it on Craigslist.

Here's an example of what a typical balance sheet might look like:

Assets:

House:	$425,000
Car(s):	$12,000
Investments:	$235,000
Savings accounts:	$2,300
Furniture and other household items:	$7,000
Employer pension plan:	$63,000
Total assets =	**$744,300**

Liabilities:

Mortgage:	$200,000
Car loans:	$6,000
Credit card debt:	$1,300
Total liabilities =	**$207,300**

Net Worth (Assets – Liabilities) = $537,000

In the assets column, list all the material things you own, such as your house, car(s), boat, cottage, artwork, antiques, jewellery, etc. Then list all the intangibles, like bank accounts, savings, brokerage accounts, business interests, stock options and anything else you could turn into cash if you had to. If you don't have an actual statement from a financial institution for these, estimate as realistically as you can.

Next comes the less-fun part: listing your liabilities. Drag out your statements and add up everything you owe. This includes your mortgage, line(s) of credit, credit cards, student loans, personal loans, family loans, unpaid taxes and all other outstanding debts (yes, even all those lovely things you rashly bought at one of those "Don't Pay A Cent Event" deals that let you buy now and pay next year). All these things represent cash you have to give back sooner or later.

Now comes the moment of truth. The first number is everything you own, and the second number is everything you owe. The difference between these two numbers—your liabilities subtracted from your assets—is your personal equity, or "net worth." Hopefully, this number isn't negative. Having good personal equity is the holy grail of financial planning, and the most important element in it is usually the equity in your house. When the value of your house goes up and your mortgage stays the same, your personal equity rises. If your house value declines, your equity follows it down. But since those matters are often outside your control, it's best to focus on what you *can* control, which is learning to spend less than you earn. If you do that, you add to your assets faster than you add to your liabilities.

From the thousands of people we've advised, we estimate that maybe five per cent—that's just five clients out of every 100—actually know where their money really goes. Even fewer accurately track both their spending AND their net worth. Yet cash flow and net worth are the starting point for all successful planning.

If you've followed our advice and created a set of goals and values (Chapter One), then completed your cash flow spreadsheet and balance sheet (this chapter), take a moment to congratulate yourself, because you've made a great start on the path to becoming financially fit!

You've performed the financial equivalent of consulting your doctor to determine an appropriate baseline from which to begin. Now, it's time to start the sweating and suffering in earnest, as you learn how to increase your financial fitness from that starting point to Olympic calibre.

As with improving your physical fitness, becoming financially fit probably won't feel good at first. There are all those old bad habits to change, and you'll be flexing mental and emotional "muscles" that you aren't used to working out. At times, you might even wonder if the end result will be worth it.

Take heart: after conversations with thousands of grateful clients, we can tell you that the rewards of financial responsibility far exceed the challenges. We're confident that, by the time you finish this book, you'll agree.

Summary of Chapter Two

- For both financial and physical fitness, you need to know what your baseline is.
- Your physical health can be determined by a visit to your doctor who runs through a checklist. Your financial health requires you to create a cash flow statement and a balance sheet, which forces you to create your own checklist.
- Our modern consumer society wants to siphon away your wealth by encouraging you to spend unconsciously. So foil the demon debt, and become aware of your spending at all times by tracking your cash flow.
- Two numbers are crucial: how much you *earn* every month, and how much you *spend*. Your entire economic well-being depends on the first number being larger than the second.
- A vital piece of information is how your assets stack up against your liabilities. Create a balance sheet to establish the value of your personal equity.

To get the most out of Chapter Two, complete the following exercises:

1) Cash Flow Analysis

The secret to financial Nirvana is positive cash flow. The number you spend has to be smaller than the number you earn.

The **www.copperjarsystem.com** website offers you a simple spreadsheet to track your spending. Pull out the credit card statements and bank statements from last month and enter the amounts in the spreadsheet. Complete at least one month, but entering the last two or three months would be even better.

The spreadsheet will add up your expenses and subtract them from your income, to allow you to fill in the following essential equation:

My spending in the last (month/two months/three months) was:
$ _____

My income in the last (month/two months/three months) was:
$ _____

Result:

- I have positive cash flow = give yourself a well-deserved pat on the back.

- I have negative cash flow = prepare to do whatever is necessary to get to positive cash flow, and save your financial sanity.

2) Balance Sheet

This is the statement that shows you what you own and what you owe. Using the **www.copperjarsystem.com** spreadsheet or any other spreadsheet that you prefer, pull out a list of your investments, the value of your house and anything else that represents an asset you could turn into cash. Enter the current value of each asset (what you could sell it for today) on the appropriate lines.

The liabilities column is for anything you owe. This includes credit card balances, lines of credit, mortgages, car loans and so on. Enter these items under liabilities.

Once you have a cash flow statement and a balance sheet, you have your baseline and the foundation for all future planning.

Your Current Net Worth Statement

Assets	Owned by You	Owned by Partner	Jointly Owned
Liquid Assets			
Bank Accounts:			
Stocks:			
Bonds:			
Deposit Certificates:			
Subtotal:			
Semi-liquid Assets			
Notes:			
Pension Plans:			
RRSPs:			
Business Interests:			
Subtotal:			

Real Estate			
Residence:			
Other:			
Subtotal:			
Personal Effects			
Household Items:			
Furnishings:			
Car(s):			
Other:			
Subtotal:			
TOTAL ASSETS:			

Liabilities	Owned by You	Owned by Partner	Jointly Owned
Personal Liabilities			
Accounts Payable:			
Credit Cards:			
Loans:			
Unpaid Taxes:			
Mortgages:			
TOTAL LIABILITIES:			

Summary	Owned by You	Owned by Partner	Jointly Owned
Subtotal-Liquid Assets:			
Subtotal-Semi-liquid Assets:			
Subtotal-Real Estate:			
Subtotal-Personal Effects:			
TOTAL ASSETS:			
Subtotal Personal Liabilities:			
TOTAL LIABILITIES:			
NET WORTH (Assets – Liabilities):			

CHAPTER 3

Getting a Baseline

If you're like most people, you likely have problems with that deceptively simple activity known as "focusing." We mostly mean well. But in our hectic modern world, it can often be difficult to stay on track with our goals.

For example, there are all kinds of challenges that can prevent you from getting into better physical shape. You're a busy person, and it can be hard to find the time to get to the gym regularly or participate in your favourite sport. You have the best intentions for a healthy diet, but at every corner, you're faced with a seemingly endless array of tasty, unhealthy fast food. As the world keeps speeding up, it becomes harder and harder to stop hurrying along after it, and start focusing on what's really important.

Financial fitness faces the same challenges. Consider the fictional case of Sandy and Lee, a typical modern couple, both reasonably well educated and employed. They're still young-ish, but they already earn more money than their parents ever dreamed of. (In fact, people today make more than any other generation in history.) They have a house, a mortgage and no children. In short, the world appears to be their oyster.

When they started out in their careers, one of their first purchases was a car, which of course they bought on credit—after all, these days, doesn't everyone take out a loan to get a new car? The car dealer was only too happy to extend their financing over five years, so their 60 monthly payments cost about as much as buying a couple of Starbucks coffees a day. It didn't look like a lot of money. But if Sandy and Lee ever stopped to analyze what they were actually paying for that car (which probably cost more than their parents' first home), they'd realize that the interest component of that monthly payment is colossal.

Thanks to that "hidden" cost, by the time they actually own the car, they'll have paid considerably more than the original sticker price.

Making Unconscious Spending, Conscious

This simple story illustrates a problem many of us have with our spending: a lot of it is unconscious, or at least not thought through. We do it out of habit, or because it's what everyone does, giving little or no thought to how our choices impact our financial well-being.

For example, Sandy and Lee mentally calculated their car payments in terms of daily cups of coffee—in North America, practically a universal tradition. How many of us pick up a cup of java on our way to the office? After all, it's only $4 or $5, right? At lunchtime, you hit the cafeteria or your favourite local eatery, where a sandwich and drink will cost you another $5 or $8. Together, that's about $10 to $15 a day. Multiply that by 230 working days, and you're out a whopping $3,450 a year, just for lunch and your morning Joe.

What other options are there? You could start your day with coffee at home, and keep the kids company while you're at it—or at least make the coffee there and pour it into a travel mug to drink en route. You could lower your standards and drink the office coffee during the day. And you could bring your own lunch from home, in the time-honoured tradition of "brown bagging."

Just doing these few simple things could reduce your out-of-pocket costs to around $2 to $3 a day, which would work out to an extra $200 a month. If you used that extra cash to pay down your mortgage, you would save tens of thousands of dollars in interest charges.

We talked about Sandy and Lee's car. Now, let's take a look at their house. Since lenders tend to be welcoming of upwardly mobile young couples with good jobs and credit records, they were able to buy their home with only a small down payment. They got a long-term amortization period of 25 years because, of course, the value of real estate always goes up. They also both expect their salaries to increase over time as they become more successful, so everything should be just fine.

But things have a way of never quite turning out exactly like we expect. Take the recent meltdown in the financial markets. The reasons behind the meltdown were numerous and complex, involving poor judgment, false assumptions and a certain amount of shifty dealing throughout the financial system. Suffice it to say that the major reason for the sub-prime crisis was that too many people used their home equity (and low interest rates for borrowing) to fund their discretionary spending, to the point where the amount they borrowed against their homes ended up exceeding the house's actual value. They also ended up with what economists call a "negative savings rate," which in plain English means spending more than you make. It's like trying to lose weight while taking in more calories than you burn off. The math just doesn't work.

As we mentioned before, you don't put on weight all at once, and putting on debt is pretty much the same. If you're spending $1,000 a month more than you earn, in five years you'll be $60,000 in debt. The worst part is all the extra dollars you'll have to shell out to service the debt. Industry research shows that by the time desperate consumers get around to considering the final resort of bankruptcy, most are carrying $2 of interest and penalties for every original dollar of debt.

In other words, they've dug themselves into a hole that's three times deeper than it had to be. Dollars of debt are like pounds of body weight: the more you have, the harder they are to shed. The extra burden of interest and penalties makes it that much harder to break out of the vicious downward cycle.

"You Deserve a Break Today"

Obviously, this is a negative spiral that *you* don't want any part of. But today's culture doesn't make the path of financial virtue easy, any more than it makes health and physical fitness easy.

Temptation is all around you. We're bombarded with marketing promises that everything can be—no, **must** be—effortless, fast and fun. We want it all and we want it now! In fact, our lives are so pumped up with speed that even the slightest delay seems intolerable. We've all seen the commercials that show a driver filling up his car at a gas pump, annoyed because it takes a whole 30 seconds to process his credit card. Meanwhile another, savvier consumer whips out his "fast, convenient, automated!" gas-station pass to pay, and is thus spared the unbearable half-minute delay. Apparently, in today's world, the distance between misery and elation has been reduced to about the time it took you to read this paragraph.

One contributing factor to this "hurry up" mentality is that most people today work much longer hours than their parents did. The average employee now works 55 hours a week, up from 44 hours in 1992. It's not unusual for young professionals like Sandy and Lee to work 60 or even 70 hours a week. This creates not just fatigue and impatience, but also a strong sense of entitlement. When people work that hard for their money, why shouldn't they get some pleasure out of it?

McDonald's introduced into the language the insinuating phrase: "You deserve a break today." The problem is, most of us aren't satisfied with the relatively minor indulgence of a burger and a soft drink. We want to go out for an expensive restaurant dinner after a rough week; we want to spend a weekend at the spa; and we always want more toys, stereos, TVs and expensive cars. In essence, we want to buy ourselves something special. We feel we're entitled to it, and the beauty is that we can pay for all of it—with the help of those ever-obliging credit cards.

It's tempting to put the blame on others, whether they be those purveyors of credit, the businesses that compete for our dollars, or the marketers who are constantly pitching their products at us. But let's not forget who bears the ultimate responsibility for our lives. Like those realtors in Chapter One who managed to overlook their kids in their seventy-hour workweeks, many of us have also accidentally mislaid our core values by chasing after convenience and instant gratification. One of those conveniences is our modern aptitude for evading personal responsibility. Today, it seems, there are plenty of victims and few culprits.

So how can well-intentioned people break out of this negative spiral? They can start by going back to the beginning. In both our financial and personal lives, we need to back up to the starting line and get reacquainted with first principles. One encouraging fact we've noticed is that a sane financial life usually "spills over" into your personal life, and vice versa. Sadly, the reverse is also true, as insanity in your financial life is often a symptom of a chaotic personal life. This is particularly true for couples, who often turn against each other when money matters go awry. There's a real temptation to blame the other person for the disarray, pointing a finger at that new car he insisted on buying or the daily cleaning lady she couldn't live without.

The reality is, in most cases, both partners are guilty. Either or both may have reservations about the financial wisdom of the trip to Paris, but neither wants to deal with it. When one person does things and the other permits them, it's what psychologists term "enabling." Your goal is to recognize that you both have a responsibility to keep your finances on track because, ultimately, we each bear the final responsibility for our own well-being.

Know Your Limits

One way to restore sanity to our financial lives is to know our limits, and make a conscious choice to respect them—rather than unconsciously spending too much, as we so often tend to do. We need to take charge of our lives and actively move toward the goals that suit us, rather than allowing ourselves to be swept along on the current of spending too much, working too much, eating too much, and ending up somewhere very different from where we really want to be.

We live as the lottery winners of mankind, having in our possession every gadget or toy imaginable. Yet it seems our major worry is always money. Many of the clients Paul and Alan see are overscheduled, over-stressed and often broke, regardless of how much money they make. All this takes its toll on our psyches. Depression is at an all-time high in modern life, as are physical ailments like allergies, obesity, diabetes, cigarette-induced cancers, stress-related strokes and other diseases caused by our increasingly unhealthy lifestyles.

If our lives are really out of kilter, the adjustments we have to make are not minor ones. If you discover, as Alan did, that you're spending $3,000 a month more than you earn, it's not an easy situation to get out of. Like so many others before him, Alan realized that not only did he need to cut his expenditures by three grand every month, but he also had to pony up to pay for his previous excess. Those credit debts just sat there, like the hangover from a party that went on far too long.

In terms of weight loss, dropping five pounds requires only a few small lifestyle tweaks, but losing 50 pounds means a major overhaul. If you want to be healthy, you have to do what's healthy. If you play basketball and your knees start to hurt every time you jump, the first thing a sensible person does is stop playing basketball. Switch to yoga or cycling instead. Health means stopping what's hurting you, and doing what helps you. The same advice applies to our finances. Call a halt to the vicious circle, and stop spending more than you make, right now!

Obviously, this isn't a simple task. Your entire lifestyle is geared to the way you're living now, so you may not be able to change it without taking some drastic steps. To get off the credit merry-go-round and make yourself solvent again, you might even have to do the unthinkable, like trade in your big house for a smaller one, change your job or relocate your family to a less expensive community.

Not surprisingly, few people are keen to do any of those things. Having become very comfortable in their grooves, most people are reluctant to change their ways. Discussing their financial circumstances with our clients, we hear again and again that they simply can't make any adjustments in their expenditures—that everything they spend money on is absolutely essential.

Separating the Luxuries from the Necessities

This reflects a simple but insidious fact of our modern society. Over time, and with the increasing sophistication of technology, many things that were once considered luxuries have now taken on the appearance of necessities.

A perfect example is the telephone. Once upon a time, when they were first introduced, individual telephones in private homes were considered a luxury. Ordinarily, people would share a party line, or go to a central location in their town to make a call. Now, you'd be hard-pressed to find someone who doesn't consider having a cell phone with all the latest and most snazzy gadgets a basic human right.

These "essentials" can become a big drain on our income. In fact, depending on how networked they are, it's not uncommon for many people in our culture to spend upwards of $1,000 a month or more on such services as television, cable, Internet, telephones and cell phones.

It's not just that life today is so different from previous generations, either. Let's get a little international perspective on the topic of necessities versus luxuries. Several years ago, Paul was on a business trip to Moscow, and he was fortunate enough to have a young guide help him with the language, show him the sights and tell him all about life in Russia. One aspect of that life was the places they called home.

In the inner cities, many of the older buildings (formerly the grand homes of the wealthy Russian bourgeoisie) have been converted into small flats. These aren't the conventional apartments that we see in Europe or North America. They tend to be just one large room where a couple or entire family lives their lives. Typically, these units are no more than 500 or 600 square feet, and that includes the living area, sleeping area and cooking facilities. If we compare that to the standard North American condo or townhouse, our accommodations start to look positively palatial. Clearly, these two cultures have deep differences in what they perceive as the basic standard for space and amenities.

Don't get us wrong—we're not grimly advocating that everybody should live in a cave and eat only berries and roots in order to provide for their retirement. But it *is* important that you understand exactly where, how and why you're spending your money, particularly if your current lifestyle exceeds your income.

You can't save for the future if you're running a deficit, and the reality is that many people today are extended far beyond their means. Easy credit creates the illusion that we can have it all, but this illusion crumbles as we get older and realize we've mortgaged our future to pay for the present. Financial fitness is about knowing your limits.

Counting Your Hidden Calories

So what do you do now? How do you progress from here?

The first thing is to be very harsh with yourself in terms of analyzing your expenditures. First, break them down into categories—household, childcare, consumables, etc. Then, apply the point system we've established to distinguish between real necessities and unnecessary luxuries. We believe our point system (which we'll explain shortly) works because it treats the concept of "necessity" as a sliding scale.

Some things, for example, are obviously either necessities or luxuries, like food versus a vacation home in The Bahamas. But other things aren't always so clear cut. Some expenses are not quite necessities, for instance, but they're also not quite luxuries, either. So we're asking you to treat outgoing dollars like incoming nutrition, and to do the financial equivalent of counting your calories. Some are allowable, others are bad for you. To decide which is which, you have to keep track of everything you spend, and then weed out the undesirables.

As you look over your spending, what you're trying to do is identify which expenditures are actually causing your deficit. You're looking for the economic equivalent of "hidden calories." You may correctly identify some things as being necessities, but it's possible that you're still spending too much on them. Even no-brainers like housing, food and clothing can easily migrate into the "luxury" category if you're not careful. Yes, you need a roof over your head; but not necessarily a two-million-dollar mansion with seven bedrooms and a swimming pool. You need to eat, but not always at the swankiest joint in town. And while clothing is a basic necessity, a closet full of Prada or Armani isn't.

The same paring-down philosophy can be applied to other aspects of your budget as well. A hobby is one area where people often overspend. A professional cabinetmaker can justify a basement full of top-notch woodworking machinery; a weekend wood-shop dilettante can't. Similarly, Lance Armstrong needs a very different bicycle than either Alan or Paul (much as they might hate to admit it). To get fit, you don't need a membership at an expensive gym; the YMCA works just as well.

How do you decide what's essential and what's just nice to have? We recommend analyzing whether the expenses in your categories are far in excess of what you need to survive. Once you've sorted out the necessary from the luxurious, you can work on ways to get back on track. Just as switching from a knee-stressing exercise to a more gentle one will eventually build up your joints to the point where you can use them pain-free, you should also start doing things differently in the financial sphere.

If you're lucky, your financial situation may not require any dramatic action. You may already have the flexibility to make the adjustments you need to your lifestyle. But if you find yourself really stuck, it's time to throw everything onto the table. If you have a partner, ask for their input on how you can get out of this mess and live the way you want.

To make those decisions, you need to go back to your personal values. For instance, does your family mean a lot to you, but your job keeps you away from them for long periods of time? Maybe you need to change jobs, and learn to live on less than you do now. Are you stuck in a dead-end job because you don't have the skills or training to get ahead? Maybe you need to sell the house, buy a duplex, rent out half and put the money you save towards improving your education.

Find Your Inner Ski Bum!

Here's a quirky example of where life can take us.

Alan counts among his friends an adventurous couple named Rick and Patti who, one day, decided to quit their well-paying jobs, take all their savings and spend their lives skiing. Rick and Patti made a pact that they'd sample all the winter resorts they could find, and wherever they found the best skiing, that's where they'd settle down. They put aside all other considerations, like the practicality of their quest and the likelihood of them both getting good jobs at the place they chose. Their goal was just to live somewhere with great skiing.

After many fun-filled months of travel, that place turned out to be the little community of Fernie, British Columbia. Back then, Fernie was just a mining town with a great ski hill. Today, tourism has taken off, and it's now a great ski town with a minor in mining.

Rick and Patti's plan worked out. Rick found work as a skiing guide and part-time teacher, and Patti is a designer of log homes. They're doing well, and recently bought a house close to the ski hill. More importantly, their lifestyle now reflects the way they want to live—and they have great skiing almost at their doorstep.

While we don't necessarily recommend that you make that dramatic a change (though it sure sounds like a pretty good life!), this story illustrates that it **is** possible to put everything on the line and risk making some bold changes in your life. After all, if you're not where you want to be anyway, why not go for the gusto, and aim big and high?

To get started, try this exercise: take the five top goals that you set for yourself in Chapter One, go to your cash flow sheets, and see if you can identify how much money you actually spent on those goals. You might be surprised by the disproportion. For instance, you may have listed your family as your number-one priority, but still skipped out on a vacation this year because you couldn't afford it. You might have identified getting fit as important, but still ended up spending more on a new TV than you did on gym memberships.

If you find (as most people do) that you spend the most money on your house, ask yourself—does that fit in with your goals? Which is more important to you: owning a big house, or financial independence? Is having two expensive cars the way you most want to spend your money? Is the job that lets you pay for those cars keeping you from seeing much of your family? Is this the way you want your life to be?

Please note that we're not judging you. There's absolutely nothing wrong with spending all your money on a big fancy house, if that's what you really want. Similarly, there's nothing wrong with working 72 hours a week if that's what's most important to you. The Copperjar System™ isn't about telling you how to live; it's about asking you to focus on how YOU really want to live, and helping you get to that point. Spending all your money on your house is only a problem if you'd rather be spending it on something else.

Let's get back to the point system we mentioned earlier, and we'll show you how it works. Look at all the expenditures you've listed, and rank them on a scale of 1 to 10—"1" being absolutely necessary for your survival, and "10" being a complete luxury. When you've got them all tagged, look at all the "10" items, and no matter how much you may be attached to them, cut them mercilessly out of your budget and your life. (We warned you this part might hurt.) If that doesn't balance the books, move on down the list to the "9" items, then the "8"s, and so on.

Keep doing this until you reach the point where your budget breaks even. Then go a bit further, and you'll find you're now at the stage where you can finally put aside some savings.

A Tale of Two Cash Flows

People can spend similar amounts each month, yet have very different priorities reflected in their expenditures. Consider the examples below of two very similar—but very different—families.

Monthly Expenditures	Bill and Tracy (Family of 3)	Fred and Emily (Family of 2)
Mortgage:	$2,200	-----
Utilities:	$350	$350
Movies:	-----	$150
Eating Out:	$200	$500
Sports:	$500	$400
Food:	$1,800	$1,800
Medical:	$150	$1,800
Clothing:	$300	$220
Telephone:	$550	$300
TV:	$80	$80
Dentist:	$100	$400
Property Taxes:	$500	$750
Newspapers:	$50	$80
Internet:	$200	$100
Music:	$100	-----
Electronics:	$100	-----
Savings:	$1,000	$1,000
Retirement Plan:	$1,500	$1,500
Holidays:	$1,200	$2,500
Car Payments:	$600	-----

Monthly Expenditures	Bill and Tracy (Family of 3)	Fred and Emily (Family of 2)
Maintenance:	$200	$200
Gas:	$250	$300
Tuition:	$500	-----
Total:	$12,430	$12,430

Let's look at some of the differences—some reflect age and stage of life, some reflect circumstance, and some are choices that are made.

Bill and Tracy:

1. Have a mortgage and lease a car, so they have two loans to pay.
2. Spend on sports instead of entertainment.
3. Have lots of communication costs.
4. Pay tuition fees for their child(ren).
5. Spend less on holidays.
6. Have employer-sponsored health and dental care.

Fred and Emily:

1. Have paid off their mortgage and have no interest payments.
2. Own vs. lease a car.
3. Spend more on entertainment.
4. Don't have tuition to pay.
5. Aren't as healthy as Bill and Tracy or don't have an employer health plan.
6. Have a more expensive house.

As you look at the list, you may see opportunities for these two families to make changes or cut expenses. The value in knowing your expenses, the way Bill and Tracy or Fred and Emily do, is that you can step back and assess whether or not your monthly spending truly reflects your goals and priorities. Once you know where your money goes, you can begin trimming expenses. If you are in negative cash flow, some of the cuts are going to be painful.

The hardest part of this process, of course, isn't just *planning* those to-the-bone cuts; it's actually *inflicting* them on yourself.

Summary of Chapter Three

- Switch from unconscious spending to conscious planning.
- Our culture encourages us to borrow money today, spend it tomorrow and only pay it back far in the future. Be wary of living on borrowed time and money. Remember, interest rates fluctuate and personal priorities shift.
- "Little" things can add up to a lot. Figure out what luxury items you're treating as essential, and scale them back so you can live within your means.
- If you need motivation to downsize, try to be inspired by other cultures that are less materially fortunate than ours.

To get the most out of Chapter Three, complete the exercises below:

1) Moving From Unconscious to Conscious Spending

My top five goals are:

1)

2)

3)

4)

5)

I spent $ _____ on my top priority last month/year.

I spent $ _____ on my 2nd priority.

I spent $ _____ on my 3rd priority.

I spent $ _____ on my 4th priority.

I spent $ _____ on my 5th priority.

Are you spending your money on what's important to you?

2) Ranking Your Expenditures on our Point System

Take your completed cash flow sheets from the previous chapter and see which categories of expenditures seem higher than they should be. Pay particular attention to categories that are not consistent with your top five priorities. Which of the items in these categories can either be eliminated or reduced?

CHAPTER 4

Planning for Retirement

Let's say you're 16 years old and out of shape. It's relatively easy to improve your level of fitness, right? Not that it isn't a struggle. But you have the time, you have plenty of opportunities to engage in physical exercise, and your body is still ready, willing and able to do what you want it to.

How about if you're in your 20s? A little tougher, maybe, but still no real problem. How about your 30s? 40s? 60s?

Getting financially fit is a lot like getting physically fit. The earlier you start—and the longer you've been practicing good habits—the "easier" it is for you to make a change. If you've exercised hard all your life, for example, and paid attention to your state of fitness, your situation is very different from that of a "late starter" who only gets around to contemplating their future when they hit middle age.

Sadly, Paul and Alan see all too many people who fall into that kind of position. The worst part is, one of the most common reasons they're there is bad advice from so-called financial experts. A lot of the bad planning that happens (or worse, *doesn't* happen) these days is from financial advisors who use formula-based plans that they don't really understand. That kind of "planning" is worse than useless, because it often leads people to throw up their hands in despair or the belief that they'll never get a serious handle on their financial lives.

Like contractors who make a steady living putting right the damage inflicted on people's homes by the incompetent or unscrupulous, conscientious financial managers are often distressed to see how many people's personal finances are made needlessly stressful or difficult by listening to the wrong kind of counsel.

The Curious Case of George and Carolyn

Consider the case of George and Carolyn, a successful couple in their mid-50s who were earning a combined income of $250,000 a year. Their home was paid off, as were their debts. Their two kids were in private schools. And they had almost half a million dollars saved in various retirement plans and mutual funds. They were both contemplating retiring early in another decade or so, and felt the time was ripe for a detailed financial plan.

So they picked a planner at random from the Internet, and went to see him. This planner asked them a few brief questions about their circumstances, and how much income they'd need for retirement. Since that was what they were there to find out, they truthfully said they had no idea. Quite accustomed to this response, the planner said he'd assume a "rule of thumb" figure of 75 per cent of their current income.

Let's take a moment and briefly step aside from this conversation.

What is the reason for "rules of thumb" in financial planning? A rule of thumb is there to take the place of valuable, personalized information. It takes time to produce a cash flow and balance sheet. But this work is the foundation of any reasonable plan, and simply assuming it away destroys any value your "plan" might have had. Please do not make the same mistake and assume the work involved in creating a cash flow statement and balance sheet can be replaced by a rule of thumb. You are just wasting your time if you do.

Certainly, the financial planner in our example had little or no interest in spending the time required to figure out George and Carolyn's cash flow and balance sheet. In fact, there is a very good chance that, as with many "planners" today, the creation of a financial plan may not be his primary objective. His primary objective may be the sale of a financial product.

In our opinion, a real plan is worth paying for, and it is independent of any product sale. A proper financial plan does not assume a generic figure for how you will live when you retire, and it certainly requires you to create a proper balance sheet.

Let's return to the conversation between the planner and George and Carolyn. The planner's next question was about their tolerance for investment risk. "How much can you stand to lose in a year?' he asked.

George and Carolyn just looked at each other. "Um, nothing!" George replied somewhat hesitantly.

"Very well," the planner said; "we'll categorize you as 'risk-averse.'"

So the planner entered these snippets of information into his financial-planning software, and after a few nanoseconds, out came the answer: "According to these figures, you'll need to save another seven million dollars before you can retire." The program also helpfully provided a schedule for their savings, requiring them to put away about three times their current annual take-home pay each year for the rest of their working lives.

George and Carolyn left the planner's office feeling completely discouraged. They had been under the impression that they were doing pretty well. This financial planning exercise showed them that their retirement was a lost cause, and saving for it was clearly a pointless exercise.

Top Three Mistakes to Avoid

When we heard this tale of woe, we immediately spotted three huge problems with what transpired:

1) The couple hadn't done any homework in terms of finding a competent planner. They hadn't asked their family, friends, neighbours, colleagues or relatives for word-of-mouth recommendations, and they hadn't shopped around to see what different approaches might be available. As a result, not surprisingly, they suffered the same fate as inexperienced consumers in any field: they ended up with a dud.

2) They'd gone in almost completely unprepared. George and Carolyn should have shown up with a briefcase full of all their financial files, including our old friends the cash flow spreadsheet and balance sheet. If they'd taken a look at their own figures first, they'd have realized that they were in fact in very good shape, and that any "expert" who told them otherwise needed to have his head examined.

3) The planner based his advice on a faulty set of assumptions. When he plucked that magic "75 per cent of current income" figure out of thin air, he completely overlooked some extremely important factors. For example, in ten years, when they were planning to retire, the couple would no longer be paying those hefty private-school fees, or even university tuition, because their children would have graduated by then. As well, a big part of their monthly expenses was the savings they were so conscientiously socking away. But the planner neglected to point out the rather obvious fact that saving for retirement stops at retirement. If those things had been factored into the equation, the math would have changed dramatically. In fact, George and Carolyn already lived quite modestly, and would continue to do so in retirement—without the mid-life expenses they'd paid for so long. Rather than still needing three-quarters of their current income, a more accurate figure would have been about 40 per cent.

The irony of the situation is that this financially responsible couple, who were actually right on track for their retirement, trusted this bad advice, got their limits wrong and, as a result, became utterly discouraged. They felt they'd failed, even though they were really on the brink of success. How many other professional advisors could manage to convince their clients of such a counterproductive thing? It would be like going to see a personal fitness trainer because you wanted to get into better shape for your weekly volleyball game, and instead being put into a training program for Olympic athletes. The point here is that any competent advisor should ask you what your goals are, and you need to be able to tell him. If you don't know, you have to clarify them for yourself. But if you *are* clear about your goals, you're in a good position to get meaningful advice.

As we keep repeating, the best way to keep your financial fitness in good shape is to regularly examine your cash flow. Track your cash flow for at least several months, and you'll begin to get a sense of which expenses will stay in retirement and which will go. As we just pointed out, two categories that can be removed from the equation are your savings and your children's education. Once those are gone, you just have to identify the core living expenses that remain, and you'll have a realistic post-retirement income to aim for. (Keep in mind that in addition to your own pension and savings, you'll also be entitled to government benefits and pensions.)

"I've Done the Math the Way You Said, But I'm Still Short!"

We used the example of George and Carolyn to illustrate the point that bad advice can scare off even people who are in good shape financially. Sadly, not everyone is so fortunate. Some people have either never made a serious attempt to save money, or they did try, but life tossed them a few curve balls. Either way, they don't have enough savings to retire and still maintain anything like their current lifestyle.

Financial fitness is about understanding your limits. Physically, people with supposedly crippling disabilities manage to do incredible things with their bodies, like wheelchair athletes who play world-class basketball or hockey. There is even an Olympic sprinter with no lower legs. Their physical limitations didn't stop those athletes, and your financial limitations shouldn't stop you from preparing for your retirement as responsibly as you can.

Your first step is to figure out how you can start accumulating as much capital as possible. If you're 50 and in debt, then get out of debt and start saving. We know that's easier said than done. But it's also essential. Now is the time to throw all your cards on the table, because you have nothing to lose and everything to gain.

Let's say you have 10 years left until retirement. After making some dramatic lifestyle changes, you figure you can put away $2,500 per month. That's $30,000 a year, and $300,000 over 10 years, without taking into account any income earned on the money you save. Assuming you invest your savings at the very modest interest rate of four per cent, you'll end up with an annual income of about $12,000. Assume, again, that your government benefits amount to another $12,000. This means that, in your retirement, you'll be living on $24,000 per year.

How will you spend that income? Obviously, that's a matter for you to determine for yourself, based on your personal goals and what's most important to you. But as you construct your post-retirement lifestyle according to your values and limitations, here are a few ideas you might want to explore. Some are a little unconventional, but they're all options people have actually used to keep down their single biggest expense: housing costs. The main starting point for all these ideas is selling your home and pocketing the proceeds.

- Buy a duplex and live in one half while someone else pays you to rent the other half.
- Buy into co-op housing, an attractive option for many seniors.
- Rent a small and inexpensive apartment.
- Rent a larger flat or house, and get some roommates. Back in your college years, you did this to defray expenses. If your personality type allows it in your retirement years, try the lifestyle again. (Hey, it works on TV!)

- Move to a smaller, less expensive community, well outside of urban centres.
- Buy a chalet in a popular ski resort, live there in summer, and then rent it out at a profit in the peak ski season (while *you* rent a cheaper place someplace warm).
- Move to a less affluent country, where your annual income of $24,000 is more money than most people see in a decade. (How many people have moved back to the old country to retire?)

All of these are valid options, and it's even possible to combine one or more of them in inventive ways to suit your particular tastes, circumstances and budget. We don't favour any one of these lifestyles over another; the one that's right for you is the one that best honours your values and suits your lifestyle.

What we *do* advocate, very strongly, is that you do not just drift into retirement as though you're in a canoe floating along on the current when suddenly, around a bend in the river, comes a gigantic and unforeseen set of rapids. To put it another way, don't let the end of your working life crash into you like a runaway truck that you never saw coming. You *do* know retirement is coming. You've known it intellectually at least since the start of your working life, and you've probably felt a gathering sense of urgency about it if you've passed the age of 50.

So take our advice, and make the best changes in your life that you can manage—changes that maximize your potential for a worry-free retirement.

Summary of Chapter Four

- When it comes to hiring someone to help with your financial planning, the old term "Buyer Beware" applies. Make sure you entrust your economic well-being to someone who is competent. Check them out, and check out their references.
- Prepare yourself by being on top of your own situation. Track your cash flow for a few months to get a realistic picture of your expenditures.
- Refuse to accept outrageous projections for future income that demand millions of dollars in savings.
- Keep in mind that many of your current expenditures will vanish in retirement.
- Even if life has dealt you a tough hand, resolve to take your retirement planning seriously and do what you can to follow the program.
- Remember that one major benefit of retirement is that it gives you significant flexibility, which you can use to redefine many aspects of your life and finances. There are many creative solutions, and hopefully at least one of them will turn out to be right for you.

To get the most out of Chapter Four, complete the following exercises:

1) Realistic Financial Planning

Take the cash flow sheet you prepared earlier and see which expenditures will likely go away or be reduced in retirement. The rest of the expenditures are your "core" retirement expenses.

My core retirement expenses are approximately $ _____ based on today's spending.

If your assets and pensions are on the way to supporting this figure, you are in good shape to maintain your current lifestyle through retirement. To check out the asset base and pensions required to support your core retirement expenses, use the simple retirement calculator at **www.copperjarsystem.com.**

2) Supporting a Successful Retirement

If you are not able to support your current lifestyle through retirement, you will need to make some changes. Which of the following changes are most consistent with your values and aspirations?

1) I can move to a country where the cost of living is lower.
2) I can move to a smaller, more inexpensive community.
3) I can work part-time at something I love to do.
4) I can sell my large home and buy a smaller one, an apartment or a duplex.
5) I can increase my savings rate.

These are just a few of the possible options that are available to you. The important thing to remember is that we all have the ability to change our lifestyle to something we can afford, whatever our means.

In the space below, write out the changes you could make to create a lifestyle that is within the means of your retirement resources:

_____

_____

_____

_____

_____

CHAPTER 5

Setting Up Your Financial Fitness Routine

Every fitness program requires discipline and routine. If you want to get physically fit, you have to start by deciding to do it, get some medical advice to make sure it won't kill you, and then set up some type of activity schedule to accomplish your goal.

Typically, you start out slowly, and over time your workouts get both more intense and more sophisticated. Eventually, you may get so enthusiastic that you begin to explore more advanced options, like running, cycling, yoga, aerobics, swimming, marathons or even Ironman races. You may also recruit professionals who can help guide you, such as a nutritionist for diet advice or a personal trainer to help you get the most out of your workouts.

Financial fitness is no different. When you first start, "just the basics" will be all you really need or want. Try to do too much too soon and your plan will suffer for it. Health clubs profit significantly from the flood of determined New Year's-resolution keepers who line up every January 1, prepared to get fit and slim down. But in their enthusiasm these people often start too fast, ignore the rules for safe workouts, and get too tired or hurt. By the time February rolls around, they're generally back on the couch, convinced once again that fitness is not for them.

That's why, when it comes to your financial fitness, it's important to have a routine. Start at your own pace, do things the right way and gradually work your way up to more sophisticated financial challenges. Over time, as you get good at it, you can expand your routines to reach your longer-term goals.

If you've been following this book conscientiously, you've already acquired several useful tools to control financial chaos. You've defined your values and key goals, created your cash flow spreadsheet and balance sheet, gotten a good idea of how much money you have and how you spend it, and come to realize that, if you've been spending too much on the wrong things, it's time to change your spending habits and live within your means. If you've done all that, there's light at the end of the financial tunnel.

Saving Money and Building Equity

Now it's time to turn our attention to the next stage of financial fitness: saving money and building personal equity. How do we get started? By going back to the "first potato chip" rule of setting goals, and doing one thing that gets you moving in the right direction. As the physicist Sir Isaac Newton postulated, bodies at rest tend to remain at rest, while bodies in motion stay in motion. Financially, you want to be a body in motion, moving in the direction of personal economic sanity.

Once you break that initial inertia and take the first step, it will often have a cascade effect. In physical fitness, for example, you might start by walking a single block, work your way up to a long walk and then, before you realize it, you're running long distances.

When it comes to your finances, what's *your* first potato chip? We recommend you start with your debts. Begin to pay them down instead of running them up. Remember our example from Chapter Three, about the basketball player with the injured knee? Take heed of that principle. Stop doing what hurts you, and start doing what makes you get better.

Right at the top of every debt-reduction strategy is credit card debt. Let's face it, most credit card companies charge interest rates that all but guarantee you'll stay in debt for the rest of your life if you don't pay off your outstanding balance. Rates of 18 to 21 per cent are common, and some charge even more. So start off by getting rid of this debt.

Review your credit card statements and write down the interest rate each one charges. Check the rate on your car loan and write it down, too. Do the same for your line of credit and your mortgage. Write them all down, line them up from highest to lowest, and then see how you can shift as much debt as possible from high-interest to low-interest loans.

If your line of credit charges you six per cent, for instance, and your credit cards charge 21 per cent, then move the balance from credit card to line of credit and cancel the credit card. Don't transfer the debt and keep the card! The idea is to transfer all the money you owe to the place where you'll pay the least for the privilege of owing it. Cut up all your credit cards except for just one, and promise yourself to use it only for emergencies. When you do use it, pay it off in full. Better still, look for and find a credit card that works like a debit card.

Psychologists have found that consumers tend to spend almost 20 per cent less money when they use cash instead of credit. When the bill won't arrive for another 30 days, people tend to spend more easily. Knowing this, you should make every effort to switch as much as possible to using cash (or at least a debit card on an account with no overdraft protection). Do this, and you'll likely save a small fortune every year. Paul's envelope system has the same underlying idea, by forcing him to make spending a *conscious* activity.

Kicking Your Debt Addiction

Over time, as paycheque follows paycheque and more and more of your incoming funds go to pay off those debts, your interest burden will gradually shrink and you will have more money to pay off the principal. When the happy day comes when all your cards are paid off (and it will!), set your sights on your lower-interest debts. Get rid of them, in order of their interest cost. Try to get to the point where, on your balance sheet, you have only the most basic of liabilities: your mortgage, and possibly your car payments.

Once those debilitating debts are gone, take very good care to make sure they never come back. Again, it's like physical fitness—once you make real strides towards getting fit, you want to stay that way. You're motivated to avoid doughnut shops, and when you travel on business, you check to see which hotels have gyms so you don't have to miss your workout. Just as bad habits create more bad habits, good habits also cascade into other good habits.

By the time you've paid off that last credit card, the memory of the painful withdrawal from credit addiction will be so intense—all the endless, griping pressure of trying to find more ways to cut spending at the expense of your usual pleasures in life—that you'll be willing to do almost anything rather than put yourself into that kind of situation again.

When your line of credit gets down to zero, think about calling your bank and reducing your credit limit. Being in debt tends to create more debt. When the balance on your line of credit is $80,000 or so, it's easy to spend another 10 grand. The $10,000 expense is much harder to justify when you owe nothing, and you want to keep it that way.

Along with your newfound religion of debt reduction, if it's feasible (and it may not be), you might also consider setting up a small savings plan. It could be as little as $25 or $50 per month, but even a little savings can add up quickly. Perhaps more importantly, you'll know in your heart that you've become a saver.

You may actually be surprised at how easy this can be. For instance, check out the benefits offered by your employer. Many employers will match all or part of the contributions you make to retirement accounts or employee savings plans. One chat with Human Resources and you may find that your monthly $50 in savings can turn into $100, just by asking!

Even if that's not the case, getting a modest savings plan going represents an important step in your financial fitness regimen, because it means you're moving from playing catch-up to actually getting ahead, actively charting your own course and taking back the power to make decisions over your money and your life.

Just as in your exercise program, you'll move from barely coping to gradually taking on more vigorous activities, and soon you'll be ready for new financial challenges. You've established routines, you're paying down your debts and your savings are growing. Your confidence is starting to rise, based on the positive steps you've set in motion. So now is a good time to think about the future.

What's Your Savings Target?

Once your finances are under control and you know what's practical for you right now, you've got a reasonable foundation for planning ahead. Your cash flow can tell you what your core living expenses are, and that number can be the basis for all your retirement planning.

Everyone has a "retirement income" number, usually plucked out of the air in a one-size-fits-all manner. The number is different for everyone. Some can live on $25,000 a year; others can't manage with less than $250,000. It depends on the lifestyle you're accustomed to, and the one you project for yourself in retirement. Reality may force you to adjust your number to reflect your circumstances. If so, better to do it sooner than later.

Here's our rule-of-thumb figure for calculating your savings target: you need to amass a capital amount that's roughly equal to the annual income you'll need, divided by four per cent. Why four per cent, you ask? We've chosen that number as a feasible rate of return that will likely hold through the next few decades, regardless of market fluctuations. It may go lower, and it may climb higher (even a *lot* higher, depending on how successful your investments are), but this is a feasible ballpark figure.

The four per cent figure also needs to be a "real" rate of return, meaning it must take into account the effects of inflation. If inflation is 2.5 per cent per year, for example, your portfolio will need to net an average of 6.5 per cent to give you a four per cent annual income and still compensate for inflation.

If we were to write it out like a formula, it would look like this:

(your annual retirement income) ÷ 4% = your target retirement savings

So if Mr. and Mrs. Smith feel they can live on $50,000 a year in retirement, for example, their goal would be to bank $1,250,000 in savings:

$$\$50,000 \div 4\% = \$1,250,000$$

Another way to look at it is to multiply your current or projected savings by that same four per cent, to determine how much retirement income it will generate. For example, one million dollars in savings will yield a "real" retirement income of about $40,000 a year ($1,000,000 x 4% = $40,000).

The result won't be an exact number, but it's a worthwhile starting point. You can find a simple spreadsheet to help you with the calculations on the Copperjar System™ website at **www.copperjarsystem.com**; you can refine the figure using financial-planning software; or you can visit your own financial advisor (who will hopefully be able to give you the right answer once *you* ask the right questions).

In fact, if you've followed our advice so far, you'll be one of the few people who are actually capable of having an informed conversation with their planner, because you'll know going in what you spend, where you stand and what your goals are.

Once you've got the retirement savings number you're looking for, the next step is to see what it takes to get from "where you are today" to "where you need to be in the future." If you're lucky or you've planned and saved well, you may find that you just have to keep on doing what you're doing already. But if it turns out that you're a long, long way from your goal, you may need to implement a more intensive savings plan or make more drastic changes in your lifestyle.

Whatever you do, don't fall into the trap of looking at those projections and becoming discouraged. Remember those similarities between financial and physical fitness. A walk around the block is better than no walk at all. If your projection requires you to save $1,000 a month, and right now all you can manage is to pay off your debts and save $25 per month, you're still moving in the right direction. Your target—whether it's reducing body fat or amassing retirement capital—may feel like a pipe dream. Remind yourself firmly that it *is* doable if you dedicate yourself to the goal.

Every great success story starts with a goal. Perfection can wait until you're in better shape. For now, be happy with the fact that you've made some great progress. Think of your financial fitness number like your body fat percentage—you're better off doing something than nothing. You've got yourself moving, and now you're going to stay that way!

Summary of Chapter Five

- Financial fitness, like physical fitness, requires both discipline and commitment—a series of determined actions repeated at regular intervals.
- Avoid the "New Year's syndrome" and remember that any time is a good time to start saving. Go at your own pace, doing whatever you can. Don't make excuses—just do it.
- Get serious about debt reduction. Line up the amounts you owe on your credit cards and loans by their interest rates, and pay them off accordingly.
- Start even a modest savings schedule, and find out if your work has any savings plans
- Any action that gets you moving in the right direction is good. One positive change creates the momentum for more positive change.
- Focus on the progress you've made, not whether or not you fall short of perfection.

CHAPTER 6

Building Your Personal Equity

Most books on financial planning are very big on saving as the path to wealth. They admonish their readers with sayings like "if you want to be rich, save more" or "pay yourself first!" The idea is apparently that if you sock away just a little at a time, eventually vast riches will be yours.

It's a lovely dream, but sadly, it almost never happens. Let's be clear about this happy little myth once and for all: **no one saves their way rich.** It's like trying to diet yourself fit—you can become slim by dieting, but you need exercise to be fit. Dieting (reducing your calorie intake) is certainly analogous to saving (reducing your dollar outflow). But that is only one part of a complex equation, which depends on many other factors as well. We have to be frank about this: people can save themselves comfortable, but they can't save themselves rich.

That doesn't mean we want to discourage you from saving. Quite the opposite; saving is very important. But it has its limitations, and it's essential that you have a clear idea of what can and can't be accomplished by saving. Think of people you know who are rich—for the sake of argument, let's define "rich" as being worth at least five million dollars. The chances that even *one* of those people "saved their way rich" are pretty slim. You can save yourself from being poor, but being rich takes a lot more.

So how do people become rich? Some are lucky enough to have been born into a wealthy family. Sadly, that isn't an option for most of us.

Some people get rich by inheriting, starting or selling a successful business. Others may be partners in a profitable concern, or make a bundle in real estate.

Before you abandon your savings plan and go running off to make your fortune, let's take a good hard look at the facts. Being a successful entrepreneur sounds like a great lifestyle, true. Compared to physical fitness, it's the equivalent of being a top-ranked professional athlete. There's quite a gap between being someone who's reasonably fit and healthy, and someone who's paid millions for their incredible athletic abilities.

It's the same with financial fitness. Just because you're comfortable in your job, pay your bills and save for your retirement, doesn't mean you necessarily have what it takes to be an entrepreneur.

Be on the Lookout for Equity Opportunities

So what does it take to create multi-millionaire wealth? Two simple words: **personal equity.**

If your ambition is to be rich (or at least rich-*er* than you are now), then you need to deliberately set yourself the goal of building equity. We've seen this done in many different ways. Real estate has traditionally been a good option. Some people build a portfolio of commercial real estate, acquiring properties over time as they can afford them and allowing their tenants to pay for their investment while watching the value of their properties rise.

If that sounds too ambitious, maybe you own a cottage and the one next to you is for sale. Could you buy it and rent it out by the year or season, so that you essentially get paid for owning the property? If you're willing to find out, crunching some numbers with your financial advisor or accountant could yield some very positive results.

A word of warning: real estate is not failsafe. No investment is. But if you're interested, here are a few rules of thumb when it comes to investing in real estate: first, don't overpay. If the rents don't support the valuation—pass. And second, make sure you can afford to carry the property if it sits empty for several months in a down market. Remember the painful lessons of the 2008 meltdown: real estate isn't liquid, and it can be tough to sell in a downturn.

Another option is to look for a job that offers stock or pension benefits. If you're hesitating between one job offer and another, check out the pension plan. Does one company offer a generous pension and the other not? The former will eventually yield the most equity for you. Similarly, many financially savvy people prefer jobs with generous stock options over jobs that may pay more up front, but offer less long-term equity. Would that work for you? Could you take a pay cut to get a job with a promising young company that might just make you rich with its stock option plan if the company really takes off?

Professionals can often buy into the business or practice they work for. If the company does well, it could be a major shot in the arm for you. Or perhaps you could start your own business. If there are line-ups out the door where you work and the customers are chafing because no one seems to be handling their problems except you, then you may be able to turn your job into a successful business. Most economic growth comes from energetic people who see an opportunity, follow it up and are prepared to learn valuable lessons from the experience of others. But remember: we all have to know our limitations, so make sure to match the risk with your knowledge and ability.

The main lesson we want you to take away from this chapter is to always be on the lookout for ways to increase your personal equity. The beautiful thing about equity is that it's like a field of corn—if you tend it by day, you can usually rely on it to just grow all by itself during the night. All it takes is to get that field well planted in the first place.

Have you ever wondered why, when you buy a new car, all of a sudden you start to notice how many of those cars there are on the road? It's as though they were invisible before, and then buying one suddenly opens your eyes to their presence all around you. Well, it's the same with opportunities to build equity. Once you've got the idea in your head and you start looking around, you'll begin to see opportunities everywhere.

Keep your eyes open, and you'll find that you're ready when one of those opportunities comes knocking at your door.

While you're waiting for that knock, don't neglect the everyday discipline of your financial fitness regimen. Always spend less than you make. Save as much as your circumstances allow. Pay off your debts. And remember to arrange your life in accordance with your core goals and values.

Summary of Chapter Six

* No one saves their way rich.
* Rich people have equity, and really rich people have lots of equity. They own companies, real estate, other business interests or some combination of all three.
* Start looking for opportunities in your life to build equity. For instance, when it comes to jobs, don't just look at wages and lifestyle—consider pension benefits, stock options and other ways to leverage the wealth you already have.
* If you have what it takes to be self-employed, go for it. Entrepreneurship is a great way to build personal equity.

To get the most out of Chapter Six, complete the following exercises:

1) Sources of Equity

Check off which of the following sources of equity are open to you right now:

1) Pension Plans.
2) Share purchase plans.
3) Employer-matched savings plans.
4) Self-employment opportunities.
5) Business opportunities.
6) Investment opportunities.

If you don't know whether some of the opportunities above are open to you, make a list below of what you need to investigate to find out:

1)
2)
3)
4)
5)
6)

Beside each item, list when you will investigate and include the names of anyone you need to involve to get your answers. Follow up until you know exactly what is available to you and how you might access the opportunity.

2) Pursuing Opportunities

Which equity opportunities are you willing to pursue outside your current situation?

1) Different work.
2) Entrepreneurship.
3) Investment real estate.
4) Part-time business.

Note below what you are willing to do to pursue one or more of these opportunities. Set a time for your first step and note any other people that need to be involved.

_____

_____

_____

_____

_____

_____

_____

_____

CHAPTER 7

Cutting Back: Trimming the Fat from Your Budget

From time to time, we all get nostalgic for the past—our glory days, a time that was filled (at least in retrospect) with unbridled optimism, freedom, athletic exploits and youthful romance. "Things were simpler back then," we say with a sigh. "No mortgage payments, no work deadlines, no family responsibilities. Life was easy and pleasant."

The sad truth is, once we become adults, our lives do get more complicated. With house and car payments grinding us down every month, it can be hard sometimes just to count all the bills we have to settle, let alone actually pay them. We become responsible not just for ourselves, but for others as well. As the song says: "Freedom takes on new meaning when you have a family of five." Depending on who you are, this could mean a partner, children, an extended family, a business with employees, or even an entire community.

Take Paul, for example. How have his responsibilities changed as he progressed through his life?

"When I was in university, I thought studying for exams was as stressful as things could possibly get," Paul recalls. "Then I graduated, got a job with a law firm and became an articling student. That was much harder, but I took comfort in the certainty that surely everything would get easier from there on. Then I finished articling, became a lawyer and found out that not only did I need to work hard at my job, I had to find clients as well! When I was made a partner, in addition to all those burdens, I also had to worry about the firm."

Finally, Paul and a partner opened their own law firm. "Now, I have to know the law, find clients, worry about the firm—and also be responsible for what everyone else is doing. From this vantage point, I look back on those student days as positively carefree!"

Adult life is complicated not just socially, but economically. Our personal finances acquire a complexity undreamed-of in the days when we lived at home, borrowed our parents' car whenever we needed transportation and enjoyed the fruits of our summer jobs without giving a second thought to bills or what the future might hold in store. Being an independent adult certainly has its rewards. But greater rewards always come hand-in-hand with greater responsibilities.

Shifting back to our fitness metaphor, professional athletes face a similar change in their challenges. They may start out as simply gifted natural athletes, whose passion for their chosen sport keeps them coming back to the rink, ballpark or playing field at times when the rest of us are home in bed. But as they become more skilled and better trained, they begin to compete more seriously, and at higher and higher levels. The bar of their personal best keeps moving and, as a result, they have to train longer and harder. Everything in their lives has to support their quest for athletic superiority—what they eat, where they live, how they sleep, and what other activities they can engage in. If they want to be the best, they have to stay focused on their athletic goals 24 hours a day, and not allow themselves to be distracted by anything.

It's the same with our financial lives. We all face challenges that are, in their own way, every bit as daunting as those faced by professional athletes. To be successful, we need to get everything aligned, focus on our personal goals and make sure that all our efforts support our core aims, whether that be paying down debt, starting a savings plan or increasing our personal equity. None of this happens by accident, just as no athlete finds his or her way to the podium purely by chance.

All too often, we engage in behaviours that are the financial equivalent of a fitness buff sneaking off to the doughnut shop for a couple of chocolate éclairs. We justify it to ourselves by saying that it's a small reward for all the daily stresses we have to face. Yet these little indulgences so often put us at odds with our larger objectives. Instead of bringing us peace of mind, they actually move us away from our true goals.

Granted, a minor doughnut-shop misdemeanour once in a blue moon won't kill you. It's a small setback, from which you can easily recover. But if your goal is the financial equivalent of a gold medal, you can't let yourself get sidetracked too often. Getting in shape and staying in shape means no more stops at the doughnut shop on the way to your workout. It's the same financially. If your budget is stretched out of shape, if you find yourself unable to reduce your debt or meet the savings target you've set, it may be time to take a good hard look at the reasons for it.

The True Cost of Indulgence

For example—what does your cash flow look like? Are there any indulgences that aren't contributing to your goals? There are any number of pleasant and enticing ways to shoot yourself in the foot. Do you (or your partner) spend inordinate amounts of money on clothing? Do you love to entertain, and have a monthly food-and-drink budget the size of the Gross National Product of a small country? Are you addicted to home improvements, and never happy unless you've got a new project on the go? Are you a travel nut who likes to reward yourself for a hard year's work by taking the family to an exclusive Caribbean resort?

All these indulgences can look like legitimate expenditures, until you engage in some serious financial soul-searching. Let's face it, most of us have limited means and unlimited desires. But if we want to avoid a financial meltdown, we have to learn to live within our incomes. If you really long for less complicated times, here's the solution: make your life simpler. Trim the fat from it. Focus on the long-term goal, not the short-term temptation.

Think about it: does that pricey vacation really contribute to your long-term well-being? If you can afford it and still meet your savings target, great. But if you are in a negative cash flow, chances are that as soon as you get home again, that luxurious getaway is going to sit on your credit card statement (and your mind) like a two-tonne weight. Why not try a family camping trip that costs only a few hundred dollars instead? You'll probably still have a great time, plus you'll have the satisfaction of knowing you've lived within your means and contributed to your mental peace and self-confidence.

Try this exercise: using your cash flow sheet, flag the top five discretionary expenses that you think you could live without, and still honour your core values.

Expense 1:
Expense 2:
Expense 3:
Expense 4:
Expense 5:

Now—how would you feel if you cut each of those expenses *in half?* Would it be too painful for you to adjust to a 50 per cent cut in your travel budget, or make your next dinner party a potluck? How would you feel if you reallocated that money towards reducing your debts or realizing one of your life goals? What's the "first potato chip" that could get you moving?

Cash-eaters: The Silent Killers

While we're talking about trimming the fat from your expenditures, it's possible that you're feeling a bit panicked. You may look at your cash flow and say to yourself: "I'm not one of those big-spenders with their fancy cars and luxury vacations. I live pretty lean—but I *still* have no money! I'm doomed!"

If that sounds familiar, take comfort in the fact that you're not alone. You're most likely simply suffering from a problem that afflicts the vast majority of North Americans. We call it "cash-eater-itis." Although you might think you're in good shape financially, you may actually have a whole whack of "cash-eating assets" chewing a big hole in your financial future. Cash-eating assets are assets that belong on the credit side of the balance sheet, but which actually erode your financial well-being every day you own them.

Picture this scenario: you're trying to get into better shape. You watch what you eat, you go to the gym every day and you're working on losing a few pounds and getting your body feeling fit. To help you along, you buy some dietary supplements that are supposed to boost your metabolism and help you slim down. But after taking the supplements for a couple months, you discover that they're really sugar pills, and instead of helping you lose weight, they've actually been packing on the pounds!

You work out, watch your diet, do all the right things—and then, *by a combination of accident and poor research*, those pills undo all your hard work without you even being aware of it. You think you're making progress, when in fact you're slipping backwards. Surely nothing could be more discouraging.

In our financial lives, we compromise our current and long-term financial well-being all the time—and we do it on purpose and with great enthusiasm. In fact, it happens almost every time we choose to make a large purchase. We may view such purchases as assets, but the truth is that they create hidden liabilities.

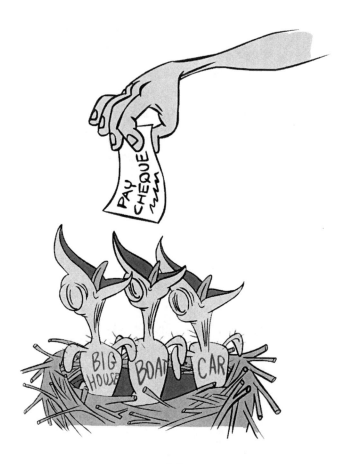

How can you tell the difference between a real asset and one of these cash-eaters? The defining characteristic of cash-eating assets is that you need to feed them dollars on a regular basis, because they cost you money each and every month you own them. Here are some examples of a few of the more common cash-eaters you might have lurking hungrily around on your balance sheet:

- House
- Cottage or vacation home
- Timeshare
- Car
- Boat
- Recreational vehicle
- Fine art
- Antiques or collectibles
- Cell phone
- Computer

At this point, we can imagine you're jumping to your feet with outrage and shouting: "Are you guys out of your minds? A house is the best possible investment—and besides, you have to live somewhere!"

Agreed, we all DO have to live somewhere. But have you ever heard the expression "house-poor?" Being house-poor is defined as spending more than 35 per cent of your take-home pay on all the combined expenses of your house: mortgage payments, taxes, insurance, heating and cooling costs, upkeep, utilities and so on. If you're over that magic one-third mark, then it's possible that you, like so many other people in our society, are living in too much house.

Cash-Rich or House-Poor

Most of us go through pretty much the same pattern when it comes to buying houses. Our first house is generally a modest "starter home," and it's a great source of pride regardless of how many bedrooms or stainless steel appliances it has. As our families and paycheques get bigger, we steadily trade up to larger and larger spaces. Granted, our home equity usually keeps growing as well. Unfortunately, it doesn't always keep pace with the higher mortgage payments and property tax bills, the larger rooms to furnish, and the more costly upkeep.

The same can be said of your cottage, if you buy one. True, it may well appreciate in value; but the costs associated with owning and maintaining it—insuring it, winterizing it, replacing the old septic tank, dock, roof, pump or boat, and entertaining all the "friends" who descend on you for visits all summer long—probably far outstrip its dollar value.

The same pattern repeats itself with other consumer goods. Take that most beloved of all North American obsessions: the family car. Most people in our culture upgrade their cars every few years. This costs more, either up-front or in monthly payments. Either way, you also give up all the investment income that cash could have generated, or else you pay interest on the debt you owe for your shiny new gas-guzzling beast. If you're really dedicated to the joys of motorized mobility, you may also buy an ATV, snowmobile, RV or even a boat. (Yachting, by the way, has been described as standing in the rain burning $100 bills).

As we become more affluent, we tend to regard it as only natural to buy more cash-eating assets. This is how we advertise our success. The trouble is, you can only carry so many of these "assets" before you go broke. You can only afford so much house, make so many car payments or acquire so many electronic gadgets. Earlier, we talked about lottery winners and professional athletes who make millions and then go bust. Such people often make the mistake of allowing their cash-eating assets to silently undo all their good financial fortune. We make a habit of acquiring stuff that *looks* like an asset, but which actually destroys the good work we're trying to do.

The opposite of those pernicious cash-eating assets is cash-*producing* assets—assets that add to your personal equity rather than detracting from it. A savings account is a good example. The more savings you have, the better off you are. An income-producing investment property is another. Whatever form they take, you can own an unlimited number of cash-producing assets, and always be better off for it.

If you're struggling financially, the obvious solution is to replace as many cash-eating assets as possible with cash-producers. You caused the situation, so you can fix it. You were the one who first brought these cash-hungry monsters into your life. Now you're stressed, broke, in debt, and unable to honour your goals and values. It's time to look the monster in the face and deal with the cash-eaters that are hiding in your financial attic.

Get Rid of the Cash-Eaters in Your Life

Thankfully, there are a number of tools we can use to help us corral these beasts and get them back under control. One is the balance sheet form we've designed to help you with this exercise, which you'll find on the Copperjar System™ website. This form divides your assets into two categories: cash-producing assets and cash-eaters. Your goal is to rearrange your life so that the first column is bigger than the second.

Go ahead and try it now. Make a list of all of your cash-eating assets. Using your cash flow statements, calculate how much money each of them takes out of your pocket every month. Start with the biggest, and work your way down the list. You can refer to our earlier examples of common cash-eaters if you need a push to help you get started.

Now that you've made your list and found out just how much each of these cash-eaters is costing you, what can you do about it? If you're house-poor, can you move into a more modest home? If you have an expensive cottage, can you rent it out whenever you're not using it, and turn it into a cash-producer? How about selling that cash-guzzling boat, and just renting one for the two weeks or so every year that you actually use it?

Don't get us wrong: we don't want you to live like a pauper, missing out on "la dolce vita" in the name of fiscal responsibility. Really, we do want you to have the best life you possibly can! We're just urging you to do so in a way that lets you live within your income and with peace of mind. By all means, enjoy summers at the cottage, entertaining friends, travelling and dining—provided you can afford it.

It's like we said before—if you're working hard to get fit, but all your hard work and discipline is being undercut by something that negates your efforts, you get discouraged. Yet in our financial lives, we're only too willing to accept the same situation. We work hard to create a good lifestyle for our families, and then undo all of that hard work just because we're not aware of the impact of our cash-eaters on our bottom line.

The lottery winners and busted sports stars broke themselves with cash-eating assets. The challenge we all face is to understand that, as the wealthiest society in history, we are all lottery winners. Now, we need to take the steps to truly enjoy and benefit from our incredible good fortune.

Summary of Chapter Seven

- Think back to the simple, happy times of your life, and learn a lesson from them. Some stress is a necessary part of being an adult. But too much stress is brought on needlessly through over-consumption.

- Become aware of the cash-eaters in your life—the assets you need to feed with money every month. The biggest of these is likely your house. If you spend more than 35 per cent of your net income on housing, you're probably "house-poor." Yes, you need a roof over your head; but not necessarily one that eats away at your financial well-being.

- Make a list of all the other cash-eaters in your life, and separate them from bona-fide cash-producing assets such as savings accounts, stock options, etc. Try to make the cash-eating list shorter, and the cash-producing one longer.

- Look through your cash flow sheet to identify anything that doesn't contribute to your financial goals. Devote some thought to re-allocating your spending from low-priority items to your higher priorities.

- Repeat to yourself this little mantra: every cash-eating asset is a step *away* from true financial independence, and every cash-producing asset is a step *toward* it.

To get the most out of Chapter Seven, complete the following exercise:

At the end of Chapter Three, you created a balance sheet to establish your current baseline. It's time to revisit that baseline.

Take a look at your balance sheet, and list all your cash-eating assets. Now, ask yourself the following:

1) Do I have more cash-eating assets than cash-producing assets?
2) How much do my cash-eating assets cost me each month?

If you have too many cash-eating assets, what tough measures can you take to reduce the monthly load they represent? In other words, which of these hungry pigs can be sold, and which can be made smaller?

I can sell the following cash-eating assets:

1)
2)
3)
4)

I can reduce or buy a less expensive version of the following:

1)
2)
3)
4)

My total monthly cash savings from taking these actions is:

$_____

CHAPTER 8

Knowing Your Limits

Alan once spent a weekend mountain biking in Utah with a dozen other guys of varying skill levels and athletic ability. After some guy-style negotiating about pace and route, the group finally broke into two packs—one that viewed itself as "high performance," and one that was more concerned with arriving at their destination in one piece. (Alan gets coy when asked which group HE belonged to.)

Unfortunately, two of the people who attached themselves to the high-performance group had over-estimated their physical capacity. Unable to keep up, they dropped behind, lost their way and found themselves stranded in the desert with little water and a temperature of 102 degrees. Through a combination of level-headedness and luck, they lived to tell the tale. But their story could have had a very different ending.

This cautionary tale shows the importance of being conscious of your limitations, whether it is in terms of your knowledge, your ability or your stamina. That's true when you're biking in the desert, and it's equally true when it comes to your understanding of **investments**: how they work, how much risk you can tolerate and your actual ability to withstand that risk. If you overestimate what you can handle and get in over your head, you might end up wandering in the financial desert, lost and alone with the vultures circling high overhead.

We're talking about investments at this point in the book because we hope that, by now, you've put some of your new skills into practice, and put aside a few dollars as the result of all your discipline. If you're still with us, we hope you've got your goals in hand, your cash flow and net worth sorted out, your debts reduced and savings increased, some of your cash-eating assets disposed of, and maybe even put a plan in place for retirement alternatives. The challenge now becomes where, how and with whose help to invest your hard-earned cash.

Your Investment Options

The most common financial advice most people receive is the old mantra of "Pay yourself first"—meaning, make sure that contributing to your savings takes top priority when it comes to your discretionary income. That's very good advice, and we encourage you to follow it. As soon as you've paid off all your credit cards.

Once your credit cards are paid off, it's time to start contributing to a savings plan and, if you own a home, paying off the mortgage. Ideally, you want to pay off your mortgage, save for a rainy day, save for the kids' education and contribute to your retirement savings, all at the same time. While this may be possible for some, most people will need to make choices between these competing priorities.

To make your choices, go back to the goals and values you identified in Chapter One. The choices that are most aligned with your goals are the choices that will give you the greatest satisfaction. You may find your goals include saving for retirement, paying down your mortgage or saving for your child's post-secondary education.

The first stop for retirement savings should be a registered retirement savings plan (RRSP). An RRSP provides you with a tax deduction against income for every dollar contributed, as well as tax-sheltered growth for the investments within the plan.

There is a limit to the amount you can contribute to an RRSP (18 per cent of your income per year to a maximum of $22,000 in 2010). Once you have reached that maximum, it's time to set your sights on one of the newest tools in your financial arsenal: the Tax-Free Savings Account (TFSA).

A TFSA allows you to save $5,000 per year on a tax-sheltered basis. There is no deduction against income for money deposited to a Tax-Free Savings Account, but you do have the advantage of not having to pay tax on anything earned within it. You can also make withdrawals from a TFSA at any time, and replace the funds whenever you see fit.

If you have children who are likely to go on to post-secondary education, a Registered Education Savings Plan (RESP) is another tool you may want to consider. An RESP allows for a grant of up to $500 per child per year, calculated as 20 per cent of the amount of your RESP contribution, up to a maximum grant of $500.

It can be a real challenge to choose between two or more worthy goals. Paying off your mortgage could be one of your top priorities, but saving for retirement is also likely to be high on your list. You may be able to honour both goals by making an RRSP contribution and then using the tax savings to pay down your mortgage. If saving for a child's education is your highest priority, you may decide to postpone paying off the mortgage for a few years while you establish an RESP.

It's important to be cautious of the distinction between plans such as RRSPs, RESPs and TFSAs that are officially sanctioned by the revenue authorities, and those that merely represent aggressive tax planning on your own part. Only sophisticated investors with experienced advisors should consider any of the latter options. If you miscalculate your taxes and get caught in a reassessment, you could end up having to pay substantial penalties, interest charges and professional fees. Savvy investing and using loopholes are all very well and good, but if you're not careful, you could accidentally find yourself on the wrong side of the law.

Striking a Balance Between Fear and Greed

In the last chapter, we spoke about finding an acceptable balance between survival and luxury. When it comes to your investments, there's another balance that's equally important: the balance between **fear** and **greed**.

We're all greedy to acquire as much as we can, and fearful of losing what we already have. Those two countervailing influences act as a natural check on each other, usually preventing us from straying too far in either direction. For instance, we might be tempted by a financial opportunity that promises an astronomically high rate of return. But if we have any sense at all, we know that if something sounds too good to be true, it probably is.

When you're considering your alternatives, it pays to be aware of the various investment options that are available. It's also important for you to be aware of a very different set of options—namely, the professional guidance that informs your selection of one investment over another. We think it's important to stress this matter, because it can make a real difference to your financial outcome, and because so many other books tend to assume that all investment professionals are interchangeable, as though competence makes no difference between one advisor and another.

Unless you're a financial expert in your own right, very few people can run their business affairs successfully alone. There are three relationships that are crucial to your financial success: your accountant, your lawyer and your investment advisor. (Another important relationship is with your partner, but we'll discuss that in greater detail later on.)

It's critical that you find reliable professionals to fill all these niches, particularly the third. Sadly, there are plenty of salesmen out there who have no scruples about calling themselves "advisors," when in fact they're really just adrenaline-pumped, trend-happy, trade yourself-silly yahoos whose main concern isn't increasing *your* money, but getting it into *their* pockets. Such people are part of your financial problems, not the solution, so make sure you don't get taken in. A *good* investment advisor understands both your knowledge level and your tolerance for risk. He or she may cost a little more, but they could also save you a fortune.

Risk vs. Reward

Let's start with the subject of **risk tolerance**.

Every advisor in the business, including Alan and Paul, have had clients who demanded that they should be able to earn the highest possible rate of return, without the risk of losing any of their capital.

In a perfect world, that might be possible. In this world, it just isn't. That's the financial equivalent of wanting to have your cake and eat it, too (and maybe have it fed to you by Megan Fox or George Clooney while you're at it). Your first aim should be to become at least reasonably educated as an investor, with a basic grasp of how the market works, and what is and isn't possible.

Paul occasionally likes to shock his friends and colleagues by claiming to have succeeded in his career by being stupid. What he really means is that he's not afraid to *look* stupid. He's never embarrassed to keep asking questions until he fully understands a given situation.

Over his years in practice, Paul has noticed that many others around him have had exactly the same questions, but they avoided asking for clarification out of a fear of looking dumb. For Paul, the only thing that's "dumb" is lingering in an unnecessary state of ignorance because you're too embarrassed to ask a question. From his point of view, it's always better to get the answers he needs than to worry what others will think about him for asking.

Paul's example shows us that it pays to ask lots of questions—and to find an advisor who'll answer them without making you feel like an idiot. For the sake of your money, it's vital that you have a good working relationship with your advisor.

Alan has observed the financial business for more than two decades, and he's noticed that the typical investor experience usually rates somewhere between "mediocre" and "disastrous." There are a number of reasons for this, which we'll go into later, but chief among them is a simple lack of communication. That's one of the reasons we've written this book—we want *you* to have a different experience.

How Good an Investor Are You?

To do well as an investor, the crucial first step is to stop fooling yourself about your capacity. In many areas of life (including mountain biking), it's amazing how many people rank themselves as being better at something than they really are. You can see examples of this all around you—at the local tennis club, for instance, where everyone seems to think they're at least an "intermediate" player, despite what the club standings might indicate to the contrary.

A recent best-selling book about North American driving habits similarly uncovered the (statistically impossible) fact that almost all drivers consider themselves to have "better than average" skills. Or just take casinos as an example. Virtually everyone who gambles regularly claims to win big, but casinos remain one of the most profitable enterprises in the history of the world—and they don't make all that money from people who win.

Are all those people not telling the truth, or are they just engaging in wishful thinking? We suspect the latter. People are always hugely attracted to the glamour of the quick buck, the lottery win, the roll of the dice—despite the fact that the likelihood of a big win is statistically smaller than that of getting struck by lightning while reciting the theme song from "Gilligan's Island."

The lure of luck is the reason why so many people fall for those investment-firm ads that try to dazzle prospective clients with talk about the spectacular returns somebody had over the last year. Keep in mind that this advertising (like all ads) is designed to sell you something—in this case, a firm's expensive services—rather than to advance *your* financial well-being.

One of the reasons many of us are so attracted to the idea of Lady Luck as a financial manager is that most of us don't do a very good job of managing our own affairs. The average investor regularly earns far lower returns than the market is capable of yielding, and often loses significant amounts of money through unwise investments—just because they don't understand the basics of the system. It's true that markets around the world are often in turmoil, but that's not the biggest problem. For most investors, the biggest problem is a lack of general knowledge about how markets work.

A major culprit in scuttling even the best-laid investment plans is the tendency not just to overestimate our skills, but also to be overly aggressive— again, just like those cyclists who headed out into the Utah hills on their own. A study of investment patterns that rated investors according to age and sex looked at investment decisions made by young men, young women, older men and older women.

The results were fascinating. The study found that of all the subjects studied, the most successful investors were older women. They tended to invest conservatively, quickly recognized when they were out of their depth, and held onto their investments for the long term—all characteristics of smart investing behaviour.

By contrast, the worst investors were young men, who displayed almost exactly the reverse tendencies. That certainly bears out Alan's own experience—he's seen that, as a general rule, young men tend to have unrealistic expectations, invest very aggressively and learn slowly from their mistakes. In fact, sociologists have found that young men tend to be over-confident in all aspects of their lives, presumably buoyed up by excess testosterone.

Remember those driving studies we mentioned a while back? Ask most men, of any age, how they rate themselves as drivers, and more than 80 per cent will identify themselves as being in the top 20 per cent of drivers. That's a major disconnect between perception and reality. There are similar statistics for men ranking themselves over-optimistically in terms of their physical fitness, their looks and their skills at various occupations—including making love. As nearly all women know, that can be a major source of masculine self-delusion.

Don't Let Financial Woes Lead to an Unhappy Home

We mention these unflattering surveys because gender disparity in investing is a fact of life—one that is particularly unfortunate for women in several ways, not the least of which is that men in North America tend to control the family investments. When it comes to the household coffers, the best potential investors (women) frequently hand over control to the worst investors (men). Not surprisingly, this can quickly become a source of marital friction.

Let's take our fictional couple from Chapter Three, Sandy and Lee, as an example. One day, Sandy comes home and tells Lee: "I've got bad news. We lost $10,000 today on that investment." Lee's response to this unhappy turn of events might depend to a large degree on how the couple discussed the investment in the first place. If one person proposed the idea, they talked it over, and the other said: "Well, if you think it's the right thing to do, it's okay with me," then the second partner may have explicitly agreed to the transaction, but implicitly reserved the right to criticize if it didn't work out.

In this case, Lee can now say to Sandy with righteous wrath: "Why did you ever make such a silly investment? You know we can't afford to lose 10 grand!" Sandy, being only human, feels defensive and peeved, having honestly believed that they'd fully discussed the issue as a couple and come to a decision together. As a result, in addition to losing the money, Lee and Sandy's domestic forecast may well indicate that a cold front is about to move in.

Sadly, we've seen this unhappy dynamic play out all too often between couples who are dealing with their financial affairs. Some can't even refrain from squabbling right in our offices, and the advisor winds up having to act as referee. It really doesn't make any difference who plays which role, but the behaviour pattern is the same: one partner abdicates on the final decision to the other, which also means that he or she gets to blame the decider if the initiative fails.

This is a perfect illustration of the old maxim: "Success has many parents, but failure is an orphan." When this happens, a financial vote of non-confidence gets passed. Sandy now feels a bit sheepish, and is reluctant to propose any more suggestions for future investments. The self-confidence needed to manage a portfolio properly is based on the clear understanding that there will always be losses as well as gains over the course of time. But that confidence is eroded by the dynamics of a marital relationship that lacks real communication around a shared investment strategy.

An even worse scenario occurs when two partners so distrust each other's judgment or resent one another's recrimination that they split their assets and manage them separately. At that point, one partner may simply abandon investing completely, withdraw from the discussion and abdicate the management of his or her half of their portfolio. This is absolutely the worst possible result, because when partners start blaming each other and stop cooperating, *portfolio paralysis* is sure to set in.

Portfolio Paralysis

In fact, paralyses of all kinds are almost endemic in our perfectionist society. How often have you seen people refuse to try an activity or start a project because they're afraid they won't do it "well enough," or that they'll fail? This is the textbook reason behind nearly all procrastination: the belief that if you can't do something perfectly, then you might as well not even bother trying.

For example, how many people never start a diet, enter a race, launch a business or run for office, just because they believe they're doomed to lose? Our competitive society has created a psychological environment that works against rational behaviour. In some aspects of our lives, competition is an appropriate or even beneficial response. But in many other areas, the sense of being judged and found wanting inhibits many people from living larger and more fulfilling lives.

The impact of this paralysis is one thing when it stops you from signing up for the office squash league. But when it begins to hinder the way you manage your financial affairs, the consequences can be much more dire.

The challenge is to remember that you aren't competing against others, or with some imaginary ideal. You're simply creating your own series of small successes to boost your personal equity. As you progress with your finances, you'll develop the ability to do more. You'll begin to set realistic targets; you'll create a record of success that gives you the confidence and skills to do more; and you'll keep raising the bar for yourself by setting new targets and aiming ever higher.

Challenging yourself to reach farther and farther applies not just to investments or athletics, but to most aspects of human endeavour. As Christopher Columbus discovered, you can never quite reach the horizon; there's always someplace farther away to sail towards. Or think of climbing a high mountain range, where there's always another peak ahead of you. Your past achievements are behind you like the slopes you've already climbed, but even when you reach the top, there are still new vistas to conquer.

That's the way it is with financial planning, and you can't be defeatist about it. Accept both partners' past efforts—whether or not they led to success—and team up for your next adventure.

Making Reliable Investments

Although most people would like to believe otherwise, we all usually get the investments we deserve. In our combined decades of trying to steer clients towards the many low-cost, sensible and diversified investment options that are available on the market, we've lost count of how many times our informed, educated and professional opinions were passed over in favour of some Internet article or newsletter touting the latest fad.

What sells best is usually whatever's new and exciting, so if the price of gold is soaring, you can bet there will suddenly be dozens of new gold funds on the market, ready for novelty-driven "investors" to sink their money into. Of course, they'll have losses when the price of gold inevitably comes down again. But no worries, they'll be just in time to take what's left of their savings and climb aboard the next bandwagon. That's the eternal quest of the amateur investor: always chasing what the market did yesterday or last year. They pore over performance records as though they really believe that history can somehow predict the future.

That's one of the most exasperating problems we investment professionals experience when teaching our clients how to pick worthwhile investments: there's just too much financial "advice" and speculation out there. The media is flooded with information, much of it ill-informed, ill-advised, loaded with hidden agendas or just plain wrong.

Here's a little-known fact about that hot tip or confidential advice you may read in the newspaper: that "new information" is in fact stale old news, something that was already absorbed and processed by the market long before the media ever caught wind of it. Newspapers and television may be able to capture breaking news, but when it comes to the financial markets, their view is almost entirely hindsight.

Have you ever noticed how the media is always hyping some new trend, and encouraging money to move into new sectors? Astute observers will note that, a short time later, that sector will just as suddenly cool, and the money must move again. This is a windfall to the "money managers" who make their living from the billions of dollars in commissions that are generated by all these transactions, regardless of whether or not they actually yield a profit for their clients.

Why should *your* hard-earned cash go to enrich *them?* The reality is, chasing the markets is an activity best suited to gamblers. And since you've made such an effort to set aside the money in the first place, gambling with it hardly seems like your best option.

With all these dire warnings about the bath you could take in wildly fluctuating markets, nervous investors might be forgiven for thinking that maybe it's best to steer clear of the whole dangerous mess altogether, and just keep your money under your mattress. We hate to break it to you, but sadly, that won't work either. In the stock market, being too timid can be just as damaging as being overly aggressive. If you just let your money sit in a cookie jar for five years, at the end of that time, it will be worth *less* than it is today, thanks to inflation.

What *will* give you reliable investment results is if you have clear goals, practice discipline, start in the right place, and invest regularly. Those few simple rules will help you make good decisions that work for you— regardless of what the markets or CNN are doing today.

Stop the Madness!

Eventually, most investors decide to take the plunge and assume that buying stocks actually is a good idea. But for many people who make that decision—particularly men, for some reason—a kind of madness takes hold, and we become determined to beat the stock market at its own game. This is the financial equivalent of a game of "Joes vs. Pros," except it's a lot more dangerous. If there's one place (other than the Utah desert) where over-confidence can wipe out the average Joe, it's the stock market.

Oddly enough, this inexplicable delusion doesn't seem to occur in any other field of endeavour. We accept that the proper place for our middle-aged bodies is on a treadmill at the gym, not out on the field in the middle of an NFL game. But there's something about investing that makes people believe that anyone can get into the game. And so we can—usually, as cannon fodder for the players who *do* know what they're doing.

Knowing this, how should we balance ourselves on the fine line between over—confidence and excessive timidity? Of the two, some degree of paranoia is the more rational response. As humans, we still have a deep-seated instinct for caution, left over from thousands of years of being at risk of becoming dinner for a hungry animal.

Even in our modern society, the financial field is still largely dog-eat-dog. But though some level of prudence is a good idea, too much can cripple you by making you reluctant to enter the fray and earn the market rates of return you deserve on your investments. You can find that fine balance by developing the skills and knowledge that will enable you to be more astute in dealing with the reverses and challenges that will inevitably occur in your financial affairs.

Here's another important aspect to consider: time frame. Many investors tend to get antsy if they're not *doing* something with their investments, forgetting that the whole point of long-term planning is that you set a strategy and stick with it, resisting the urge to tinker. Despite this fact, many plans that ought to be reviewed only once every year or so end up being analyzed on a weekly basis, with decisions based more on emotion than logic. If you want to be a successful investor, you must recognize that stocks are described as "long-term" investments precisely because that's what they are. They perform best over the long term—that is, for a minimum of 10 years.

In their tireless effort to find out what makes markets tick, some dedicated analysts have pored over financial records going back as far as the United States stock market has recorded data. Looking at consecutive five-year periods over the last 200 years, they found that stocks perform better than guaranteed deposits 75 per cent of the time. That's an encouraging statistic, but it has its flip side: the other 25 per cent of the time, stocks will do worse than guaranteed investments over a given five-year period.

In other words, it's quite normal for stocks to under-perform "safer" alternatives like bonds for periods of as long as five years. If you're not okay with that, then don't buy stocks. Here's Alan's advice, and it's very simple: if you are going into the stock market, buy index funds—and hold onto them forever. Do that, and you'll be in the top 10 per cent of all stock market investors. If you take just one thing away from this chapter, that piece of advice should be it.

"Choose an Older Guy"

One final word about the best way to mitigate the financial dangers of the market. Stop us if we've mentioned this before, but having a good advisor is critical.

Remember Rick and Patti from Chapter Three, the couple who decided to uproot their lives and move to wherever they found the best skiing? Once they settled in Fernie, Rick qualified as a certified mountain guide—an occupation not for the faint of heart, mind or body, since it demands plenty of forethought, physical strength and the ability to make life-and-death decisions in a fraction of a second. To put it mildly, being certified to take paying clients into the mountain backcountry, way off the beaten tourist track, is a very big deal. It takes years of experience and a lot of hard work.

When Alan went out west to visit his friends, his curiosity was piqued at the thought of being reduced to a quivering ball of jelly by a few days' backcountry skiing with Rick. He knew it was risky, but didn't really understand why. So he asked Rick—who was already booked solid as a guide for the entire season, with no time to squeeze in even a good friend—what qualities he should look for when hiring another mountain guide.

Rick, a man of few words, considered the question for so long that Alan thought he hadn't heard him. He was about to repeat his question, when Rick replied: "Just find an older guy."

That's it? Alan had been expecting a long list of the many excellent qualities that good mountain guides presumably had to have. But then he realized that Rick, in his usual succinct manner, had distilled the essence of the job into five words. As Rick went on to explain: "There are plenty of young aggressive mountain guides, but there are no old aggressive mountain guides."

It sounds chilling, but it's true. If you take too many chances in the mountains, eventually one of them will catch up with you. A young "high-performance" guide might get away with being aggressive a hundred times, but only needs to overdo it just once to lose his reputation, his license or his life. That was what Rick meant, and what it took to make it over the long-term as a backcountry guide: the right balance of aggression and survival.

In the financial world, if you make a mistake, at least all you lose is your money. But the principle of hiring a guide to help you navigate the dangers still holds true. Whether you're in the treacherous world of high finance, the Utah desert or the Rocky Mountains, you need someone with experience who can show you the way.

Of course, you could always acquire that experience for yourself the hard way—say, by losing all your money and having to start all over again. But wouldn't it be a whole lot easier to benefit from the experience without having to endure the loss?

Summary of Chapter Eight

- Know your limits and define your tolerance for risk accordingly.
- Your best investment is to pay off your house or be able to if you lose your job.
- Get a good investment advisor who will respect your risk tolerance and answer your questions.
- To invest successfully, have clear goals, be disciplined, buy carefully and invest regularly. Invest—don't trade.

To get the most out of Chapter Eight, complete the following exercise:

The most important aspect of an investment objective is the time frame. While most people are conscious of their objectives, they often choose inappropriate investments because they haven't considered their time frame.

An objective that has a time frame of less than five years, for example, is not appropriate for stocks or other any other equity investment, such as real estate. On the chart below, list your various objectives. Beside each one, note the time frame you've set for yourself to achieve them:

Objective	Time Frame
Retirement	
Emergency cash reserve	
Education	
Vacation	
Home improvement	
House down payment	
Business investment	

Once you've listed all of your objectives, revisit what you're willing to use as an investment vehicle to turn those dreams into reality.

CHAPTER 9

"Get-Fit" Checklist

High-level athletes lead complicated lives. An Olympic skier doesn't just show up one day and win a medal. That medal is the end result of a lifetime of preparation and commitment.

In order to reach her goal, the Olympic skier follows a path that is divided into three parts. First, she discovers she has a natural talent that is ready to be tested and explored. Next, a plan is created and implemented to manage and maximize that talent. Training regimens, self-discipline and coaching all play a part in managing this great natural resource.

Finally, the athlete that is the end product of all that training must be protected. You can pretty much guarantee that any skier who ends up on the podium has taken at least one and, more likely, several major crashes on her way to the medals. A skier will, at some point, lose control. An edge will catch, a turn will get missed or fatigue will cause her to lose focus for a millisecond or two. What happens *after* this loss of control will depend on how she, and her coaches, have prepared for this moment.

Has the athlete trained her body to react to a crash in such a way so as to minimize the risk of serious injury? Is the course protected by safety nets? Are the skis ready to release before serious injury occurs? And if all else fails, is there an emergency crew standing by, ready to help?

Your financial fitness is not so different. In the Olympics of life, you first create wealth. The level of that wealth will be determined in part by your talent, and in part by your determination and discipline.

Once you have created wealth, the potential of that wealth will be governed by how well it is managed. Wealth creation and wealth management are like athletics and coaching—different but equally essential and intertwined components of achieving the same goal.

Finally, your wealth will need to be protected. What happens should an unforeseen incident take away your control will be determined in large part by your foresight and the planning you have done beforehand. Calamities such as an illness or disability can happen to anyone. Your financial security and that of your family will depend on your advance planning and preparation.

To put it another way: where you are and where you end up will be a direct result of your ability to create wealth, manage that wealth and preserve your wealth for a lifetime or for generations to come.

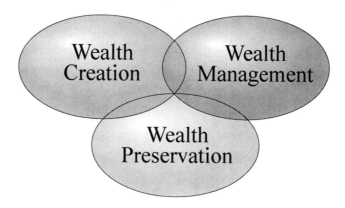

The Three Pillars of Financial Fitness

In previous chapters, we discussed various elements of a financial plan. In this chapter, we bring all the constituent parts together into an integrated whole, to give you a clearer sense of the big picture.

Take a look at the graphic on the previous page, with its three intersecting circles. These circles represent what we call the three pillars of wealth: wealth creation, wealth management and wealth preservation. Like the three legs of a three-legged stool, each of these elements is just as critical as the other two. Take one away, and the whole thing falls to the ground.

Notice also that the circles overlap. This is because each of these elements affects both of the others. Most people tend to focus on one of these elements—say, wealth creation, for example—while ignoring the others. But no matter how you look at them, all three of these pillars are equally important to you, and to your future financial success.

For the sake of convenience, the following are a few of the key issues and activities that fall under each of our three pillars:

Wealth Creation: Work and pay
Building equity
Investment

Wealth Management: Diversification
Financial education
Understanding costs and objectives
Tax management

Wealth Preservation: Risk controls
Insurance (home, life, disability, critical illness)
Wills and powers of attorney
Creditor protection

At different times, each of these elements can have a different impact. One factor that affects how they impact you is your stage of life. For instance, are you just starting out on your financial journey? At the mid-point of your career? Or are you within sight of retirement? No matter what stage of your career you're at or how your financial affairs stand right now, there are certain aspects of all three of these elements that you should definitely be thinking about.

Let's take a closer look at each of these three pillars, and the role that each of their component parts has to play in ensuring your financial success.

Wealth Creation

Work and pay

For most of us, our salaries play a big part in our financial plans. But it shouldn't be the only element you consider.

For example, we recently read about a rather unusual financial story. A cleaning woman in New York died, and left a large sum of money to a university. This bequest was all the more surprising because the woman had lived in fairly humble circumstances for most of her life, working at two or three jobs, living frugally and saving every penny she could. Whenever she managed to put a little extra aside, she invested it in bonds. Every dime she made from the bonds, she reinvested.

After a few decades of this, she had accumulated a substantial amount of money—money that she never spent on any luxuries for herself. Although this woman was technically rich, she enjoyed no personal benefit from her wealth. In fact, she lived what most of us would consider a rather diminished lifestyle. For whatever reason, the university was the ultimate beneficiary of all her self-sacrifice.

We've spoken before about how "saving your way rich" is generally not a feasible strategy. That cleaning lady is the exception that proves the rule. But regardless of a few newsworthy exceptions, we still firmly believe that saving, although a valuable discipline, is only one component of your overall wealth management plan. Think about it: for most people, the goal of wealth is personal independence; yet that woman was a virtual slave to her compulsion to squirrel money away.

Building equity

As we stressed in Chapter Six, it doesn't matter whether you're an entrepreneur, an employee or a small-business owner. There are always opportunities to create equity.

An accountant who works hard to become a partner in his firm has created equity in the partnership. The same is true for a lawyer or engineer who helps boost the practice she works for. By managing the business competently, each person builds equity. So does the employee who joins a pension plan or buys shares in an investment or stock-option program provided by his employer.

Despite popular belief to the contrary, these avenues to wealth aren't the exclusive reserve of big companies or those who are already rich and powerful. They're available to all of us.

In North America, for example, we tend to pay more attention to the companies whose names top the Fortune 500 list. But in reality, most jobs in our economy—and most of the equity they create—derive from the efforts of individual entrepreneurs. Small- and medium-sized enterprises create more than 85 per cent of the jobs, and 85 per cent of government tax revenues. In other words, small enterprise offers plenty of opportunities to build equity.

There are also a surprising number of ways to create equity other than through your employment. Dabbling in real estate is one of the most popular. Although most people's first house is a single-family home, that's not necessarily the most profitable option.

We could learn a lot from immigrants to North America, who start with a more humble goal. Instead of buying a big house just for themselves, they often start with a duplex or a small apartment building—occupying part of it as their principal residence, and renting out the rest. This allows them to begin creating equity immediately, because they own the building while their tenants pay the mortgage.

In effect, they've scaled back their lifestyle expectations in exchange for a very real opportunity to build equity. Another option might be to own a duplex while sharing the services of a management company, or pool your resources with a group of people to buy revenue properties and share the resulting equity.

An often-overlooked aspect of equity is your own individual skills and experience. Lifelong learning will soon be a critical element in maintaining our economic status. In North America's hugely competitive economic environment, a toolkit of the latest knowledge is vital to survival.

Our parents often worked at one job all their lives. But most of us can expect to reinvent ourselves three or four times in our careers. Our children will likely have to do the same thing up to *nine* times. In this constantly changing landscape, education becomes another form of equity, and a way of investing in yourself.

Whether your own your own business, or work at someone else's, what's important is for you to build your personal brand throughout your career. The value of that brand will be based on your reputation, your knowledge and your skills.

After all, no matter how good you are at what you do, you can always lose a job. Somebody can take your job away from you. An employer can lay you off. Or your team, department or company can get downsized or go out of business. But your skills are something that no one can take away from you. They stay with you, and become your personal tool kit that you can bring with you wherever you go.

When you're looking at building your personal equity, make sure you have the best tool kit possible. You want your skills to be sharp; you want them to be strong; and you want them to be recognized as valuable in and of themselves, independent of any particular job.

For instance, there is a real distinction between being an accountant who works for a company and being an accountant in private practice. It only takes one person to fire an accountant who works inside a company. The accountant with his own practice will typically need somewhere between 100 and 200 people to fire him simultaneously before his income is dramatically impacted. That is the power of personal equity.

Investment
We covered investment strategies fairly thoroughly in the last chapter, so we'll just provide you with a brief reminder here. If you are currently in debt, then the first step in your savings plan should be to stop the haemorrhaging. This means paying off your credit card debts.

Once the credit cards are paid off, you can focus on reducing or eliminating any other consumer loans you may have, followed by paying down your mortgage. When you pay off your mortgage, you're not only reducing the loss of money that's being paid out in interest charges. You're also creating equity by increasing your ownership of what is likely your biggest asset: your house. Assuming the real estate market is reasonably stable, that asset is protected by the value of your home. By paying down your mortgage, you're shifting the equity from your lender to yourself.

Once you're paying off your mortgage (or even as part of a program to pay off your mortgage), you can begin to look at other kinds of savings. Your first savings will be relatively modest, so you can probably keep them in cash or near-cash vehicles such as a Term Deposit or Guaranteed Investment Certificate (GIC). You will normally keep these savings in a bank so they will be protected by the Canada Deposit Insurance Corporation (CDIC), which protects up to $100,000 in eligible savings that are deposited in a CDIC-insured bank or financial institution.

Once your savings begin to grow, you'll want to get them working—and growing—for you. For most of us, this will likely mean investing in some form of balanced equity portfolio, which can deliver much higher long-term returns than any GIC or savings account.

As we've discussed before, when you're ready to begin looking at investing your savings, it's time to get some qualified professional advice. Ask successful friends or family members who manages their investments. Talk to several potential advisors, and be sure to ask them some of the questions in this book. Then hire the one whose experience, philosophy, approach—and, yes, personality—fits your own.

Wealth Management

Diversification
We've all heard the stories about people who made a killing from some hot stock or fad. What we don't hear quite so often are the stories of all

the people who lost everything they had when they bet it all on a single roll of the dice, and failed.

Whether it was the high-tech bubble in Ontario or the real estate boom in Calgary, Alan and Paul have seen a lot of people who became extremely wealthy just by virtue of being in the right place at the right time. In some cases, they learned from their experience and went on to become successful business people or to retire early to a life of leisure. In other cases, however, many of those who amassed their wealth through luck tried their hand at other businesses or "investments," and ended up losing a lot of money through their belief that they had been smart as opposed to merely fortunate.

What's the lesson we can take away from this? For one thing, if God gives you a choice between smart and lucky, take lucky. The truth of the matter is, the vagaries of the marketplace are such that while intelligence and hard work are often rewarded, it is not always necessarily the case. There are many intelligent people who've worked very hard and had terrible luck. There are others who coasted their way to success through little more than some incredible good fortune.

The bottom line is, life isn't fair. That's why we're such strong advocates of a diversified investment program. Diversification is a core part of almost any successful investment strategy. It is also a way to effectively minimize the long-term impact of bad luck.

What does diversification mean? In essence, it means that you invest in different sectors and industries, as well as different kinds of products (for instance, stocks, bonds, preferred shares, mutual funds and so on). By diversifying in this way, you minimize the risk that you'll end up as road kill when other people (and their money) rush from one stock or sector to another in search of the latest fad.

As you become wealthier and more financially sophisticated, you may begin to invest in private ventures. Most sensible private venture investments give you some direct involvement and participation in your investment. What private ventures sacrifice in terms of immediate liquidity can frequently be compensated by having a more controlled view and understanding of the venture.

That said, enormous amounts of money have been lost in start-up ventures. Even the most successful venture capitalist will tell you that, on average, only one or two out of every 10 investments will be profitable, two or three will break even and five or more will lose money or go under. The reason that venture capital can still be a profitable undertaking is because those ventures that are winners are often so wildly successful that they make up for the modest losses on the other investments.

Truly successful venture capitalists are also very careful in the management of their investments, and generally minimize their risk through diversification. Just remember that this is highly sophisticated, high-risk investing. Like they say in the commercials: "Performed by professionals on a closed track; do not try this at home."

Financial education

Most people bring in a home inspector before purchasing a house. To further boost their knowledge, many people seek out and read books or manuals that can help demystify the whole home buying process. When they're making a purchase of that size, it just makes sense to be prepared.

Yet, when it comes to investing, many people inexplicably assume that they can make similarly important decisions without the benefit of any knowledge, training or education. So how can you develop the same kind of ability when you're looking at financial instruments, as you do when you're shopping around for a new home?

Take an accounting course so that you can learn how to read a balance sheet. Take a course on finance or read a book like "Investing for Dummies." Find out the difference between a stock, a bond, a preferred share, a mutual fund, an index fund and so on. By learning these things, you'll start to understand the choices that are available to you to diversify your portfolio.

As a word of caution, always check where you're getting your information from. Is it coming from someone who is only interested in selling information? Or is it from someone who has a vested interest in selling you a particular stock, mutual fund or other investment? Banks and investment advisors put out all kinds of written material, for instance; but much of it is designed not to inform you, but to get you to buy their stocks, bonds or mutual funds.

In our case, we're not trying to sell you a service. You've already paid for the only thing we're selling—namely, the information that is in this book. You'll also notice that we're not giving you investment advice or suggesting that you should buy any particular stock or kind of investment. We're just suggesting that you should learn some basic information that will help you to more effectively manage your financial affairs.

Understanding costs and objectives

The first thing to understand about the costs and fees associated with wealth management is that there are no dumb questions. In fact, as Paul is fond of saying, the only dumb question is the one you don't ask. So don't be embarrassed. And don't be conned by the myth that if you have to ask, you can't afford it. In our experience, most successful business people not only ask, they also negotiate on virtually everything in their lives.

Oddly enough, many people in North America are embarrassed to bargain. We'll haggle over the price of a car, and we'll negotiate the price of a house. So why wouldn't you negotiate when you're buying financial services?

The things you need to know when it comes to the cost of managing and investing wealth are: what are you being charged, and what are you being charged *for*.

If you're buying a mutual fund, there are a few other questions you'll also need to ask. For example, what is the management expense ratio (MER)? (These are charges embedded inside the fund before you even get to the commission structure.) How much are you paying in commission for a particular mutual fund? Is the fund front-end loaded with a commission, so that only $90 of the $100 you have to invest actually gets invested? Or do they have trailers attached so that you get hit with a large commission charge if you ever decide to sell or transfer your funds to another investment vehicle?

No matter what investment you're looking at, you need to be conscious of your original goals, because those goals will determine what kind of instruments you should be in, what kind of assistance you'll need and what types of risks you're prepared to take. Then, hire yourself a professional, and understand what the costs might be of *not* having a qualified professional provide you with advice.

When you're hiring a professional, check them out. Find out what their style is. Get them to explain things to you. If they treat you like an idiot, take your business elsewhere. While the relationship with your investment advisor can be complicated, it should also be mutually beneficial—meaning, they make money and you make money. If you're unhappy, say so. Be clear, be forthright, set your expectations and hold them to account. And don't be fobbed off with explanations you don't understand.

Tax management

It is said that there are only two certainties in life: death and taxes. From cradle to grave, and indeed even after the grave, the taxman will always be there to take his share of everything you make.

Paul was giving a speech one day having to do with taxes, and he began his presentation with a modified version of the three lies. For those of you who may not know them, the three lies are: "yes, I love you," "I will respect you in the morning" and "the cheque is in the mail." Paul took the liberty of adding a fourth: "Hi, I'm with the revenue authorities, and I'm here to make sure you get all your deductions."

The reality is that the Tax Department's whole reason for being is to extract as much money as is legally possible from you, the taxpayer. Your job, in turn, is to diligently ensure that you take advantage of all the deductions and other credits to which you are entitled by the law. In most jurisdictions, you are permitted to organize your affairs to pay the least amount of tax possible. Regrettably, the taxation statutes and the strategies for navigating them are so complex that they typically can't be fully understood by any but the most experienced among us.

The truth is, the question of taxation could consume a whole book all on its own. There are a number of strategies involved with how you arrange your affairs, including the use of family trusts, participation by family members in a family business, and making sure that you realize all of the deductions and credits that are available. So when it comes to your taxes, you want real expertise.

Just as it is imperative to get good advice with respect to investing or insurance, it is equally important to have good advice on how to structure your affairs to ensure that you pay the least amount of taxes possible. So make sure you shop around. But don't make the mistake of confusing price with value.

Most professionals associated with income tax planning are paid by the hour. As with all professionals, a lower hourly rate doesn't necessary mean a better price in the long run. Look to people who have the expertise and experience to provide you with the most direct and effective guidance in the least amount of time.

There's no reason to be afraid of the taxman. Just hire good, experienced advisors, and don't make the mistake of "keeping a dog and barking yourself." If you hire good advisors, follow the advice you're paying them for, and if they're not up to the task, replace them.

Wealth Preservation

Risk controls

Some people are less averse to risk than others. Teenage boys, for instance, have an almost insanely high tolerance for risk—which is why so many of them are regular visitors to the ER.

There's a reason for their seemingly mad behaviour. Teenagers' brains are still "under construction" until they're in their mid-twenties. Only then does the part of the brain that controls risk assessment become fully developed. That's why, as adults, it's our job to act as their conscience and try to keep them out of the emergency room—or, God forbid, the morgue.

We adults have no such excuse. We're as mature as we'll ever be, and we're fully cognizant of the risks we take in our financial lives. That's why we're smart enough to know we need the financial equivalent of a safety helmet in order to manage and preserve the wealth we've created.

We've already talked about managing risk by becoming informed, selecting good advisors, getting control over your expenditures and understanding where your money is spent and invested. There are, however, other actions you can take that will provide protection from external events.

In practical terms, this means having insurance, a will and maybe a designated power of attorney—just in case something happens to incapacitate you.

Insurance

If you want to protect the wealth you've worked so hard to create, it's prudent to take certain steps. Especially if you're still in the early stages of your career, insurance coverage is crucial to protect your family in case of a disaster such as death, disability or accident. Proper coverage means that if you die, get injured or become too sick to work, your family will still have an income to live on and the ability to stay in their home.

If you've gone to a lot of trouble to amass your net worth, you ought to be equally vigilant about protecting it. It's that simple. Yet we're frequently amazed by how many people put off getting insurance, as though it were just too complicated to tackle. When we adopt that attitude, we're not being any smarter than those brain-challenged teenagers who go skateboarding or BMX bike riding without knee pads and wrist guards. If disaster strikes and we don't have proper coverage, our family's suffering will be our own creation.

There are many ways to assess your insurance needs, but the simplest principle is this: guarantee your family a replacement paycheque. If they're used to living on 60 grand a year, then make sure your coverage gives them that much. You might claim you're "covered at work," and it's true that many employers do offer insurance plans. But it's your responsibility to make sure you're adequately covered.

We've seen far too many people with families who refuse to get disability insurance because they have group coverage at work, only to discover once they get injured that their benefit was capped at a certain level or only lasted for a year or two. The situation would be much worse if you were to die, and your grieving family realized your insurance coverage was for only twice your annual salary. That would give your loved ones just two years to settle their affairs, and start over from financial scratch.

So let's take the same steps here that we did in earlier chapters, and submit your insurance coverage for a check-up. In this case, you can administer the tests yourself. Just review your files, and fill in below all the coverage you have for life and disability insurance.

Life Insurance Coverage For Our Family

Who's Insured?	For How Much?	Who Gets the Money?

Disability Coverage For Our Family

Who's Insured?	What's the Monthly Benefit?	When Does it Start?	How Long Does it Last?

Now that you have those facts and figures in hand, you can decide whether or not you have enough coverage. We usually recommend that your life insurance coverage should be at least 10-15 times your annual salary. So if your pay is $50,000 a year, the minimum amount of life insurance to aim for is $500,000 (10 x $50,000). That kind of coverage will cost a 45-year-old, non-smoking woman in good health about $40 dollars a month.

Disability insurance is a good deal more complicated. Rather than trying to explain all the intricate details and assorted options here, let's simplify matters and just say that, in case of a disability, you should have at least 60 per cent of your paycheque covered. If you don't already have this much coverage in place, it's time to see an insurance professional to assess your needs and make sure your family is protected.

A word of warning: finding a good insurance professional can be just as hard as finding a good investment advisor. Remember those rules we outlined in Chapter Eight about mountain guides? You're looking for someone with experience, since experience translates into someone who has already made mistakes, and learned from them. You need to find someone who's seen all the challenges, and learned the hard way how to create a reliable safety net for you and your family.

Wills and powers of attorney

When it comes to your family finances, a will is one of the most important documents you can have. Depending on your situation, if you were to die, a will could save your family members a little heartache and stress, or a lot.

Here's an analogy from one of our own favourite sports—basketball. Let's say that you've scored front-row seats to a hotly anticipated championship match between two of the best teams in the country. You're settled in and can't wait for the game to start. But just before the first jump ball, the referee tells the coaches to play this game without any rules. When anything happens, they'll just let everyone fight about what took place and what should be done about it.

Can you imagine trying to get a resolution to even the slightest disagreement, let alone a major foul? If the teams even get onto the court, the most likely result would be fights, injuries—and very little action.

If you die without a will, this is exactly what could happen to your family. One of the cruellest things you can do to your grieving loved ones is to leave this world without a will. That means that they're starting a game without any rules and with lots of potential for conflict and acrimony—all at the worst possible time, when they're still in mourning for their loss.

No matter how peaceful you may think your extended family is, you don't know what they might find to fight about. The result could be that those loved ones you leave behind may end up never even speaking to each other again. It has happened many, many times before, and it could happen to you. Is that the final legacy you want to leave to your family?

A will provides explicit instructions about your financial wishes. Without a will, you're surrendering your estate to lawyers and the government, and giving them the right to decide what's best for your family.

The situation is almost as bad if you *do* have a will, but it's out of date or poorly prepared. Instead of a smooth transition of family funds, you end up with stressful and expensive court battles. So do everyone a favour. Spend the money to have a proper will drawn up by a professional. The up-front expense will more than pay for itself in the savings to your loved ones in both cash and grief. Establish the ground rules before the "game" begins, and the players and referees (your family members and their lawyers and advisors) will all know where they stand. It makes the task of sorting out your estate according to your wishes easier, and allows everyone to get on with their lives.

In addition to completing your will, give some thought to selecting a power of attorney. If you are not dead, but are no longer legally able to manage your own affairs, the courts will appoint someone as power of attorney to act on your behalf and in your interest. You should therefore plan for this contingency well in advance, so you can choose someone you truly trust.

Here's another practical tip from our long experience in mediating family matters: *never* keep your will or power of attorney in your safe deposit box. Yes, it may seem like a good idea to keep all your valuable documents together in one place. But if you're dead or incapacitated, no one else will be able to retrieve your will or power of attorney designation, since they'd need those documents to access your safe deposit box in the first place! Instead, leave copies of those important documents in several different but safe places, such as your confidential files at home, at your office and with your lawyer.

To find out how prepared you are in the event of death or disaster, try answering the following questions:

Your Will

1) Do you have a will?
   Yes _____ No _____
2) Is the executor of your will aware of his/her status?
   Yes _____ No _____
3) Has your will been updated in the last five years, or since the last major change in your circumstances?
   Yes _____ No _____
4) Do you know where your will is physically located?
   Yes _____ No _____
5) Do your family members know where to find your will?
   Yes _____ No _____

Your Power of Attorney

1) Have you appointed someone as your power of attorney (POA)?
   Yes _____ No _____
2) Is the person you appointed aware that he/she may have to act on your behalf?
   Yes _____ No _____
3) Will your POA be required to act for you in matters of your personal care?
   Yes _____ No _____
4) Does your POA know where to find your legal documents?
   Yes _____ No _____

Proper planning in respect of a will can also reduce death taxes and provide for a more efficient transfer of wealth from partner to partner, or from generation to generation. It would be a shame to have solidified your financial affairs, only to let them fall victim to unnecessary taxes.

Creditor protection

The simplest way to protect yourself against creditors is to always pay your bills in full and on time. Unfortunately, that isn't always possible. So you need to structure your affairs in a manner that affords you some level of protection.

Certain assets, for example, are exempt from seizure by creditors. For instance, Registered Retirement Savings Plans that have a life insurance component are exempt from seizure. Life insurance is normally exempt from seizure. There are also thresholds with respect to which assets can be seized. Assets such as a principal residence that is jointly owned are afforded some degree of protection, as the courts are generally reluctant to force the sale of a property by one joint owner to satisfy the debts of the other.

There are also a number of simpler arrangements you can make. For example, if your occupation is high-risk, it may be a good idea to have your principal residence held by your spouse or in a Principal Residence Trust. This will help protect your home from creditors, while the law ensures that your spouse cannot dispose of your matrimonial home without your consent as long as you live there.

As your investments grow or take on greater risk, you may want to consider using a limited liability company, which will provide some protection in case the investment fails. Similarly, when investing in a company, look for vehicles such as shares or a loan rather than a partnership. This will help limit your liability for anything greater than the amount of your investment.

Techniques like family trusts or the division of assets between spouses are also legitimate and consistent ways to protect your assets from creditors. Of course, there's a big difference between structures that isolate and define the amount of loss you can incur, and structures that are designed to avoid legitimate obligations to creditors. The first is a legal and prudent approach to investing. The second enters a grey area that could cost you a great deal, or even put you on the wrong side of the law.

This is another area where good professional advice can help you set up your affairs in a manner that is perfectly legal and perfectly appropriate, but which provides some measure of protection against unforeseen risks, accidents or liabilities. For situations such as business risk, there are also insurance products available that will allow you to protect your personal assets.

Summary of Chapter Nine

- Creating, managing and preserving your wealth are all equally important aspects of your overall financial fitness
- The first step towards becoming financially successful is creating wealth. For most people, this includes our salaries, building personal equity and investing our hard-earned money wisely.
- Building equity should be one of your first goals after you stop the drain of unnecessary spending. Look at the equity opportunities around you that you can control while limiting the risk.
- When it comes to managing your wealth, make sure you understand how the different types of investments work, what costs are associated with each and what the tax implications might be.

- No matter what investment approach you adopt, always make sure you are diversified. Diversification can save you from losing everything you've worked so hard to build if a particular stock, sector or company goes under.

- Once you've dealt with the fundamentals of your financial situation, protect the result. Make sure you are properly insured—not too much and not too little.

- Pay your taxes but do your best to keep them to the legal minimum. Remember: tax planning is a legitimate endeavour. Tax evasion is not.

- Have a current will and power of attorney, and keep them up-to-date and stored in a safe but accessible place.

- Finally, hire good advisors and make them a permanent part of your network.

CHAPTER 10

Are You Financially Fit?

"Most men lead lives of quiet desperation."
- Henry David Thoreau

We've spent the last nine chapters identifying a program that will help you take control and ownership of your financial fitness. If you skipped the previous chapters and jumped right to this one in the hope that it will contain a simple, magic solution to all your financial problems, then we have some good news and some bad news.

The good news is that this chapter does indeed provide an overview and summary of the entire book. The bad news is that it's not an effortless, nine-step program with a series of silver bullets that will instantly solve all your problems. The Copperjar System™ is just that—a system. In order for the system to work, there is a program that needs to be followed. That program requires discipline and dedication (if not necessarily obsession). It requires a degree of living consciously, being aware of what you do, and understanding how each of your spending or saving decisions affects your overall circumstance.

You may think that the Copperjar System™ is only for the financially challenged, but that couldn't be farther from the truth. In fact, the Copperjar System™ is intended for everyone except those who are either wealthy enough to already have a complete system in place, or uncommonly organized enough to already be in full control of their financial affairs.

Let's look at an example of how anyone—even a finance professional—can benefit from the lessons contained within this book. As Alan and Paul were writing the first draft of what would become *The Copperjar System™*, it became both a refresher course for them as well as a place to exchange ideas, not only for the manuscript, but also about their personal lives.

Between the downturn in the economy and sending one of his children off to university, Alan noticed that his disposable income had dropped significantly. For the first time in his life, Alan was faced with having to take some of his own advice. Interestingly enough, what he did was adopt a variation on Paul's envelope system. This made it relatively easy for him to assume full control over the change in his finances.

This short illustration proves that the Copperjar System™ can be used by anyone as a tool for living consciously with respect to their financial affairs. Throughout this book, we've talked about the comparison between financial fitness and physical fitness. Using the Copperjar System™ is no different from creating an exercise program that works, suits your lifestyle, and helps you stay healthy and fit.

Financial Fitness Checklist

Financial *un*-fitness, like physical *un*-fitness, doesn't happen in an instant. It is a series of events that gradually creeps up on you until it becomes potentially overwhelming. In the process, it can create an enormous amount of stress, hardship and anxiety. If these stresses are not addressed, they will affect not only your financial security, but also your physical and emotional well-being.

After everything we've been through together over the past nine chapters, if you're still not sure whether or not you're financially fit, let's take a look at a series of questions that will help you determine where you are on the financial fitness scale. We'll start with the easy questions and work our way up to the more difficult ones:

	Questions	Yes	No
1.	Do you own your own home?		
2.	Do you have a mortgage?		
3.	Do you own a car?		
4.	Do you have a car loan?		
5.	Do you have a credit card?		
6.	Do you have more than one credit card?		
7.	Do you have more than three credit cards?		
8.	Do you have more than five credit cards?		
9.	Do you pay all of your credit cards in full every month?		
10.	Do you carry a balance on your credit card?		

	Questions	Yes	No
11.	If you carry a balance, does your total credit card debt exceed $5,000?		
12.	Does your total credit card debt exceed $10,000?		
13.	Does your total credit card debt exceed $20,000?		
14.	Does your total credit card debt exceed $50,000?		
15.	Is your mortgage loan in good standing?		
16.	Is your car loan in good standing?		
17.	Do you only pay the minimum on your credit cards each month?		
18.	Do you have a line of credit?		
19.	Is your line of credit gradually increasing?		
20.	Do you have any savings?		
21.	Are you living from paycheque to paycheque?		
22.	Do you know where you spend your money every month?		

	Questions	Yes	No
23.	Do you balance your chequebook every month?		
24.	Do you match your credit card receipts with your credit card statement?		
25.	Do you have segregated accounts for different purposes?		
26.	Do you discuss your financial affairs with your spouse or partner on a regular basis?		
27.	Do you both have access to your bank statements and investment statements?		
28.	Do you have lots of assets—cars, boats, cottages, televisions, iPods, cell phones—but always feel short of cash?		
29.	Do you make regular charitable donations?		
30.	Do you often fight with your partner over bills and expenditures?		
31.	Do you have life insurance?		
32.	Do you have home insurance?		
33.	Are all of your premiums paid up to date?		
34.	Are you getting reminder notices on your bills?		

	Questions	Yes	No
35.	Do you pay your bills before the due date?		
36.	Are you getting calls from creditors and collection agencies?		
37.	Do you avoid the mail or telephone because of creditors?		
38.	Do you use paycheque loans?		
39.	Do you hide your purchases from your partner?		
40.	Are you embarrassed about your financial situation?		
41.	Do you avoid going out with other couples because you can't afford to pay your share?		
42.	Do you use plastic instead of cash all the time?		
43.	Do you use a debit card most the time?		
44.	Do you use a credit card most of the time?		
45.	Have you consolidated your debts with a new loan?		
46.	Does the loan period on your car exceed the useful life of the vehicle?		

	Questions	Yes	No
47.	Have you added the outstanding balance on a car loan to a new car loan for a replacement purchase?		

Score:

1 point for each YES to Questions 2, 4, 5, 6, 7, 8, 10, 11, 12, 13, 14, 17, 18, 19, 21, 27, 28, 30, 34, 36, 37, 38, 39, 40, 41, 42, 44, 45, 46 and 47.

1 point for each NO to Questions 1, 3, 9, 15, 16, 20, 22, 23, 24, 25, 26, 29, 31, 32, 33, 35 and 43.

If you scored between 0 and 5, congratulations—you're financially fit!

If you scored between 5 and 15, you're slightly unfit financially.

If you scored between 15 and 30, you're seriously unfit financially.

If you scored more than 30, you're a candidate for a financial cardiac arrest.

The Copperjar System™

The Copperjar System™ isn't complicated. It isn't difficult. It's just discipline.

In essence, the Copperjar System™ is a process that enables you to:

1. Define your values;
2. Isolate and identify your expenditures;
3. Reconcile your values with your expenditures;
4. Identify your cash-eating assets;
5. Set your priorities and budgets;
6. Create and follow a monitoring and control process;
7. Build your personal equity; and
8. Make sure that you prudently protect your assets—and your family.

So what does the Copperjar System™ really do? In simple terms, the first thing it does is ask you to face the reality of your financial circumstances. As the saying goes, you don't want to "live your life in the pages of a magazine." You have to live the life you have, and you have to live it within the confines of your means and what's truly important to you.

The Copperjar System™ doesn't assign any value judgments to one way of spending over another. These are individual, personal choices, and quite frankly, they are not subject to criticism from anyone so long as they are consistent with your values and goals. If you choose to live in a modest home so that you are free to travel the world, that's your choice. Others may choose a big house and never travel any farther than their own backyard. The question isn't what you choose to spend your money on, but simply whether or not it is in accordance with your values, and the means you have to support them.

The second thing that Copperjar does is allow you, by isolating each of your expenditures, to take control over your own affairs. Once you become conscious of where and how you spend your money, it becomes a deliberate choice whether or not you continue to do so. In that sense, the Copperjar System™ is not unlike the way you choose what you put in your mouth. Once you become conscious of the caloric impact of everything you eat, your choices become deliberate.

As you become more aware of what you are spending and you create a budget that reflects your real value system, you will begin to see a significant change in your spending patterns and the amount of waste that occurs. Following the Copperjar System™ lets you discover what you spend, where you spend it and why you spend it. In essence, it moves the spending process from *unconscious* to *conscious*.

Much like a physical fitness program, some may use the Copperjar System™ like a training program for the Olympics. Others might use it simply to become financially fit enough to enjoy their lives. Some may want to win an Ironman, while others are happy just enjoying recreational sports. Each of us has the freedom to decide what level of fitness is necessary for our own individual happiness.

The same is true with the Copperjar System™. It's not designed to tell you what to value or what decisions to make. It simply provides you with the assistance needed to achieve your own individual objectives.

The results of following the Copperjar System™ are as striking as they are easy to identify:

1. Financial peace of mind;
2. A sense of control over your financial affairs;
3. A capacity to withstand financial shocks;
4. A reduction or elimination of family disputes over money;
5. Savings for education, retirement and unforeseen events;
6. The ability to confidently plan for succession and provide for your surviving partner and children;
7. The creation of a rational retirement plan;
8. The achievement of a values-based financial lifestyle; and
9. A sense of self-confidence, ownership and control that will dramatically improve your and your family's physical and mental well-being.

Find Your Path to Financial Fitness

Each year, advertisers spend billions of dollars trying to create a subliminal demand that will make you think that spending and luxury are necessities. But despite all this endless buying and consuming, depression and illness have reached epidemic proportions in our society.

Many of these afflictions are the direct result of excess stress. One of the single biggest causes of stress is time starvation. In many cases, people are too busy trying to earn more money (or, in some cases, trying to spend it) to focus on what really matters in their lives.

The Copperjar System™ allows you to stop, pause and assess your real needs. It will help you make decisions in the context of your needs, not because of the opinions of others, not the values of others and certainly not the advertising of others.

This doesn't mean you have to change everything about your life overnight. Even small changes, if they are followed with discipline and linked together, can have a dramatic and lasting impact on your personal and financial well-being.

The beauty of the Copperjar System™ is its almost universal application. This is not a program that is restricted only to those who have lots of money, or those who have none. It is a financial management system that can be beneficial to virtually everyone at all levels and at every stage in their lives.

We found it to be an invaluable tool for creating success in our own personal and professional lives. We trust that you will find it helpful in creating a sense of enduring financial fitness in yours.

Questions?

Need help?

Join our community and visit us at:

www.copperjarsystem.com

LaVergne, TN USA
08 April 2011
223477LV00002B/133/P